# SMART CITIES

# SMART CITIES: A PANACEA FOR SUSTAINABLE DEVELOPMENT

BY

AYODEJI EMMANUEL OKE

*Federal University of Technology Akure, Nigeria & University of Johannesburg, South Africa*

SEYI SEGUN STEPHEN

*Federal University of Technology Akure, Nigeria*

CLINTON OHIS AIGBAVBOA

*University of Johannesburg, South Africa*

DEJI RUFUS OGUNSEMI

*Federal University of Technology Akure, Nigeria*

And

ISAAC OLANIYI AJE

*Federal University of Technology Akure, Nigeria*

United Kingdom – North America – Japan – India
Malaysia – China

Emerald Publishing Limited
Howard House, Wagon Lane, Bingley BD16 1WA, UK

First edition 2022



**British Library Cataloguing in Publication Data**
A catalogue record for this book is available from the British Library

ISBN: 978-1-80382-456-7 (Print)
ISBN: 978-1-80382-455-0 (Online)
ISBN: 978-1-80382-457-4 (Epub)

ISOQAR certified Management System, awarded to Emerald for adherence to Environmental standard ISO 14001:2004.

Certificate Number 1985
ISO 14001

INVESTOR IN PEOPLE

To God
Who Made All Things Beautiful

# CONTENTS

# LIST OF TABLES AND FIGURES

## TABLES



## FIGURES

# ABOUT THE AUTHORS

**Ayodeji Emmanuel Oke** is a Senior Lecturer in the Department of Quantity Surveying, Federal University of Technology Akure, Nigeria and a Senior Research Associate with cidb Centre of Excellence, Faculty of Engineering and Built Environment, University of Johannesburg, South Africa. With more than 250 publications, his research interest is in sustainable infrastructure management (SIM), emphasising sustainable construction, value management and quantity surveying and construction in the digital era.

**Seyi Segun Stephen** is a Graduate of Quantity Surveying at the Federal University of Technology, Akure, Nigeria. He is a Social Psychology and Behavioural Sciences Enthusiast. He also has a flair for literature and his areas of specialisation are academic consultancy, psychological education and teaching. He is a Construction Manager and has authored books including Sustainable Construction in era of the Fourth Industrial Revolution published by Taylor & Francis, Routledge.

**Clinton Ohis Aigbavboa** is a Professor in the Department of Construction Management and Quantity Surveying, and Director of cidb Centre of Excellence & Sustainable Human Settlement and Construction Research Centre, University of Johannesburg, South Africa. He completed his PhD in Engineering Management and has published several research papers in the area of housing, construction and engineering management and research methodology for construction students. He has extensive knowledge in practice, research, training and teaching.

**Deji Rufus Ogunsemi** is a Professor of Quantity Surveying in the Department of Quantity Surveying, Federal University of Technology, Akure, Nigeria. He is currently the Deputy Vice-Chancellor (Academics), Federal University of Technology Akure, Nigeria. He is a Registered Quantity Surveyor and Registered Builder with research interest in cost management, procurement management and construction economics.

**Isaac Olaniyi Aje** is a Professor of Contract Management and Quantity Surveying in the Department of Quantity Surveying, Federal University of Technology, Akure, Nigeria. He is currently the Dean, School of Environmental Technology, Federal University of Technology, Akure, Nigeria. He is a Registered Quantity Surveyor with research interest in contractual arrangements and management, cost management and procurement management.

# PREFACE

Change is constant with humans. There is always the urge to move from a state to another no matter the level of comfort enjoyed at that moment. And with the client being insatiable in nature coupled with the quest to dealing with scarcity, construction professionals in the construction industry needed to act swift in order to meet the growing expectations and providing sustainable alternatives to scarcities. Surplus and reusable are the major terminologies when dealing with concepts that gave birth to sustainable development (SD). In the search for better quality of life, residents migrate at a very high rate from less developed areas to developed ones. This has however increased the pressure on the available resources present in such civilised cities. The population's growth is not slowing down soon at any moment hence the need to improve on what has been on ground. Smart cities come as a solution to the demands to the growing migrated population. The smartness of a city comes from the relationships between construction stakeholders and the citizens with general enhancement in mind as the targeted goal. It is believed that when there is a more technologically advanced society where operations are estimated and managed, there is bound to be improvements in all standards and ease of growth in social, physical and economic circumstances.

The smart city has been developed over the years and its benefits are numerous. As well as challenges and drivers that are part of its concept, the smart city framework inculcated into constructions will enhance the overall performances of cities as well as the citizens living in them. This book assists the readers in comprehending better what smart city in construction is all about. It starts by defining smart city to identifying concepts in it; also, the process, theories and models that are embedded in it are explicitly explained to give a solid basic understanding of the subject. The interaction between smart city and SD was affirmed in the context of the book. Furthermore, procurement in smart city development brings a new look to an angle presented in terms of functionality and acceptability of the smart city into construction processes even from the onset of planning to management of executions within a contract sum and duration.

As urbanisation continues to progress through several digitalisation processes, the architecture, engineering, construction and operation (AECO) industries are always saddled with delivering results due to the growing pressures within and outside the construction industry. The expected readers of the book are construction professionals in various fields; undergraduate and postgraduate students in the built environment discipline; policy-makers in the construction industry; procurement officers; government agencies in ministries, secretariats and functional integrated infrastructural project professionals; construction workers both in developing and developed countries; city and urban planners; building, civil and industrial stakeholders; value creators across several fields; individuals concerned with building a smart or sustainable city; building contractors and regulatory project personnel; financiers in terms of banks, bond, insurance companies; and local monarchs among other readers.

This book can serve as research guide, concepts and practices concerned in smart city development, construction management, SD, functionality and sustainability, and material notes for relating city development. It is of the hope that the readers will be educated and informed about the practices that are involved in smart city development.

Ayodeji E. Oke
Seyi S. Stephen
Clinton O. Aigbavboa
Deji R. Ogunsemi
Isaac O. Aje

# PART 1

# GENERAL INTRODUCTION OF THE BOOK

# 1

# GENERAL INTRODUCTION


## ABSTRACT

*This first chapter of this book tends to bring into understanding the various definitions concepts, evolutions, characteristics and many more on smart cities. These are further explained across the other chapters of the book as to the roles and functionalities of smart cities in this modern world. This chapter starts with an introductory part that briefly describes what cities hold and the idea of inculcating smartness into it. Furthermore, various definitions were explicitly defined across other sections of the introduction. The objective of this book relates the reason and solution the book aims to offer into the construction industry as a system that is not only functional but also sustainable across various professionals of the construction industry. This chapter ends with concluding part that describes the totality of what have been discussed in the course of the chapter. The research book also contains reference for further reading.*



**Keywords:** Smart policy and economy; smart infrastructure; sustainability; sustainable development; urban sustainability; urban system


## INTRODUCTION

Cities hold the potentials to allow their habitants access developmental opportunities; they are the poles that hold human and economic activities. As they grow in complexity and size, they pose a large range of challenges and problems. In cities, the level of inequalities are very strong such that if not properly monitored or managed, the negative effects of the inequalities can outweigh the positive effects. The concept 'Smart city' came into existence as a way to achieve efficient and sustainable cities through the innovations made possible through technological advancements. The notion of smart city is to execute specific projects, implement strategies that are accepted globally and that can mitigate challenges faced by an ordinary city.

Humans want change constantly from utility experienced. In simple term, the insatiable nature of man has driven the urge to improve profoundly in every aspect of development. Smart city as a sustainable upgrade of a city is expected to cater for the changes expected according to the locality of the city envisaged. With improvement experienced in every aspect of quality of life, life expectancy is surely heading towards that which is long and comfortable for the citizens and profitable for the stakeholders.

This research book is divided into six parts and 13 chapters across various sections of the book. The first part details the general introduction of the book; the second part explains the concept of smart cities as it introduces the subject to the reader; the third part expresses the involvement of smart cities stakeholders; the fourth part defines sustainable development along with its principles and definitions. The fifth part shows the involvement of smart cities and sustainable development and the sixth part details enhancing smart cities for sustainable development.

The first of the 13 chapters details the general introduction of the book. It introduces smart city to the readers for basic understanding on what the book entails. The next chapters do not only further introduce the book, they also discuss smart city process coupled with theories and models that makes up smart city. The fifth and the sixth chapters introduce the involvement of the smart cities teams into smart city practices. They encompass smart cities team members and partnership across stages of the smart city operations. The seventh chapter clearly defines and introduces sustainable development while the next chapter relates defined sustainable development to smart cities in terms of quality of life and the ninth chapter explains socially inclusive city. Chapters 10–13 detail drivers of smart cities, smart city dimension, challenges and procurement in smart city developments, respectively.

## DEFINITION OF SMART CITIES

Smart city as it were does not have a universally accepted definition. However, it has been defined over the years as the transformation from an ordinary city to that which is sustainable. Smart city encompasses the integration of technological innovations to cater for the needs and demands of the society. It aims to bring enhancement in every sector of the city's practices as it works in the phase of developing strategies that can better the quality of life and at the same time improve the environment.

Smart city comes with urban development in interactions with social, physical, human and the environment. The concept of this city relates with the built environment in bringing together stakeholders, residents and concerned individuals towards not only technological advancement in enhancing a city but also managing resources available for the use of all. Also, the concept of smart city is expressed within the transfer of data from one source to another through medium created. Information disseminated is vital to the general plan designed towards functionality of the smart city.

In a smart city, conservation of resources is of the most essentiality. Energies of all kinds and manners are distributed and sustained for use not just now but also for the generations to come. The sustainability to be conceptualised must be expressed in terms of ease and advancement in transportation, buildings, water system and other social amenities that forms a city.

## EVOLUTION OF SMART CITIES

So many authors have come up with concept for the evolution of smart cities and these includes 'Garden Cities of To-morrow' which was published by Ebenezer Howard in the year 1898 where the author stated that urbanism should be taken as a special concept, by which the less habitable places can be transformed to a more conducive environment with available opportunities. A speech was made by a French man by the name Eugene Henard who happens to be one of the first planners for the urban city whose work has been considered to be a plus to the future development of European cities, in the speech, he said:

> *My purpose is to inquire into the effect a positive change will bring as a result of modern science industry if well implemented to plan the Cities of the Future. The Cities of Tomorrow when compared with the Cities of Yesterday will be more readily encouraging to transformation. (Eremia, Toma, & Sanduleac, 2017)*

Some other authors in the early nineteenth century also referred to the concept of Urbanism as an indispensable instrument for life and the vitality of men. In the mid-nineteenth century, the concept of sustainable city which was a term used to mean the future urban development with a strong reaction from the United Nations. Later in the late nineteenth century, the concept of Digital cities became the second most popularly used word, where the term means a strong influence with the growth of the information and telecommunication technology with larger streams of data. Recently, especially in the early twentieth century, the term Digital cities has been jettisoned for a more and well-defined term which is Smart Cities. This term makes use of values which are sustainable with social inclusion, which conforms to the current change in the internet technologies.

## CONCEPT OF SMART CITIES

The concept of Smart City has to do with innovation in the city's infrastructures, services and management. There are a wide range of definitions for Smart City although a specific definition has not yet been agreed to be best. Smart cities put into consideration two trends that can be related to its main aspects. Firstly, it considers the definitions that emphasises on one urban aspect and excluding other circumstances which a city involves that one aspect of the urban ecosystem is improved upon does not mean that all other problems in the city is solved. Secondly, some other researchers opined that the interconnection for all urban aspects that takes place in real life is the main difference of the Smart City Concept. The problem in the concept of Smart Cities lies in the fact that infrastructural, institutional and social are all intertwined in urbanisation. From all indications, it shows that the concept of Smart Cities has a lot to do with proper management and development of the urban city. Smart City has infrastructures as the central piece, technology as the enabler that makes its concept possible, but the combination, connection and integration of all the systems becomes fundamental to a city becoming smart.

Cities are fast booming, their challenges are to be carefully considered to ensure social progress, population growth and economic development work together. For the fact that most of the global gross domestic product is derived from the cities does not mean everything happening there is going on without challenges.

In study by Schaffers, Komninos, Pallot, Trousse, and Nilsson (2011), the theory on what a smart city should entails details the presence of technological perception, adoption and implementation with allied components that exhibit smartness, digitalisation, intelligence and so on. Cities are not just getting bigger and transformed for now, they are being transformed to cater for the needs of the future while still living in the present. The 'smart' part of the city comes out where there is synchronisation in instrumentation, connectivity, autonomous, learning and relearning, dissemination and implementation of information, data, concepts, practices towards functionality and enhancement of relationship between the stakeholders and the citizens.

The concept of Smart City covers various definitions and this relates to how the word 'smart' has been interpreted. There are several definitions of Smart City, but until now, none have been universally recognised (Cocchia, 2014). Some examples of these blurry meanings are: Knowledge City, Wired City, Digital City and Green City, Ubiquitous City, Intelligent City, Sustainable City, etc., they all have a kind of connection politically, economically and sociocultural change. The meanings are in certain way part of the vague Smart City concept and we can say there is a kind of correlation in their meanings (Cocchia, 2014).

## REASONS FOR SMART CITIES

The need for a more developed and well maintained urban city brought about the need for a more technological and social reformation which was later termed as Smart Cities.

The idea of Smart City stemmed from the development of information communication technologies, which contributes to the redefinition of the concept of natural region. Smart city is the end result of a new, innovative idea about city and urban life. It is more pleasant, more inclusive, greener and cleaner.

The Smart City is nowadays seen like a key strategy to improve the quality of life of billions of people living in cities all over the world.

## CHARACTERISTICS OF A SMART CITY

A Smart City is characterised by some factors which include the intelligence of a city under some given set of values like legislation infrastructure to support the development economically, and also support the social effect of allowing the protection of the environment.

## RESILIENT CITY SYSTEM, ECONOMICALLY BENEFICIAL CITY

A resilient city is a city that is able to organise themselves to deal with crises, learn from the challenges and move on, this resilience challenge borrows its solution from the smart city. The resilience can be defined as the ability of a city to resist, absorb and accommodate effects of a hazard timely and efficiently.

In order to manage natural disasters in an ever increasing urbanisation, conditions that are specific to cities must be considered. Resilience does not only focus on natural hazards but encompasses occasional crises that may affect a city and endemic problems.

Cities are known to be complex, interdependent systems which are known for being extremely vulnerable to threats from all hazards (natural and endemic) and terrorism. The features which make a city desirable and smart as it were are also the features that make it vulnerable to hazards. This therefore makes such city a very good ground in which economic activities can thrive. Apart from the security assertion of this city, the ease in carrying out operations of various kinds will propel investors from different places across the universe. This is due to the benefits derived from a functional city which makes it the centre of attraction to neighbouring locals and internationals.

## OBJECTIVE OF THE BOOK

In identifying challenges and benefits of smart cities in the totality of its functions, several researchers (Giffinger & Gudrun, 2010; Shooshtarian & Ridley, 2016; Nam & Pardo 2011) had worked quite a lot in bridging the knowledge gap of both the citizens and many stakeholders. Other related publications can be found in journals, research books, conference papers and so on.

This research book will therefore identify with aspects that affect the implementation of smart city into the construction industry in peculiarity. This book will also address concepts and practices that can be channelled into various functions towards achieving sustainability. Furthermore, it will enhance the knowledge of the construction stakeholders to what stands to be benefitted not just now but also in the future when smart city is fully adopted and implemented into the industry. As this book serves as a research guide to individuals concerned with sustainability and enhanced construction, it can be employed to function as additional inputs to students, researchers in terms of concepts discussed already and the introduction of procurement of smart city.

## CONCLUSION

It is very essential to have solid background study of what cities are and the smartness integrated into the system as a symbol of developmental representation further what has been used to. Cites are designed to function towards essentialities but are also limited in terms of functions and peculiarities. These and many more are considered in implementing smart city concepts and practices into the construction industry. It might take longer period of time before this idea is fully implemented in most cities, it is however a matter of seeing the benefits attached to the adoption and flexibility offered in the system. In all, the citizens (public) should be well enlightened about smart city and the functions it tends to ascertain if it is fully implemented in the society.

## REFERENCES

Cocchia, A. (2014). *Smart and digital city: A systematic literature review.* Geneva: Springer International Publishing.

Eremia, M., Toma, L., & Sanduleac, M. (2017). The smart city concept in the 21st century. *Procedia Engineering*, *181*, 12–19.

Giffinger, R., & Gudrun, H. (2010). Smart Cities Ranking: An Effective Instrument for the Positioning of Cities. *Architecture, City and Environment*, *4*(12), 7–25.

Nam, T., & Pardo, T. A. (2011). Conceptualizing Smart City with Dimensions of Technology, People, and Institutions. Proceedings of the 12th Annual International Conference on Digital Government Research, College Park, MD, USA, June 12–15. doi:10.1145/2037556.2037602.

Schaffers, H., Komninos, N., Pallot, M., Trousse, B., & Nilsson, M. (2011). Smart cities and the future internet: Towards cooperation frameworks for open innovation. Lecture Notes in Computer Science. *The Future Internet*, 6656, 431–446.

# PART 2

# CONCEPT OF SMART CITIES

# 2

# INTRODUCTION TO SMART CITIES

## ABSTRACT

*The first chapter of this book has already introduced smart city concepts and definitions; the second part will further explain deeper how smart city comes into being and the frameworks that surround it. Firstly, history of city and smart city gives a detailed analogical insight on the transformation from city into smart one. The rate at which the transformation process is implemented depended mostly on how the citizens of the city understand the implementation of digitalisation concepts through the use of appropriate technologies into running and developing a city. Secondly, there are also further definitions on the subject especially as they related to the construction industry. Characteristics of smart cities are also discussed along with features that can really make a city smart. In conclusion, the chapter is well introduced and provisions were also made at the end in terms of bibliographies that will help in further understanding of the smart city concepts beings introduced.*

**Keywords:** Smart environment; smart infrastructure; sustainability; sustainable development; urbanisation; urban cities

## INTRODUCTION

There have been different development in the construction industry and has been a development process in this generation, this development has been introduced to so many countries globally, and their benefits are immeasurable. The construction sector as Smart city as one of the new innovations or developments. According to Albino and Dangelico (2015), the issues of smart cities have been discussed in the academics literature and research since 1990s. Nevertheless, the innovation of smart cities is a collective idea that have been constituted for future real city development, there is need to understand what a city is first before determining if the city can be smart.

There are various definition of city, United Nations (2016) define city as area where large numbers of people lives, transport from one place to another, a commercial centre that is been governed with right royalty and good government. According to Mori and Christodoulou (2012), they stated that city play significant roles in the life of people and their environment having dealing with social, economic and environmental development of the country. Smart cities comprise three factors are the technology factor, human factor and institution factors for the benefits of the people and their communities.

## CITY AND SMART CITY

In rising urbanisation poses great opportunities, treats and challenges to the people and on the environment, in as much as cities continue to grow, the inhabitants' demands and needs must be met in such a way that goes on well in the immediate environment. Cities consume the largest portion resources especially fossil energy thereby making resources such as disposable land, clean water and fossil energy limited for use. To maintain a long-term high standard of living, establishment of environmental landmark and substitute to unavailable fossil resources in cities is very important. Established urbanised centres need to control their development, to support economic competitiveness and at the same time enhance environmental sustainability, communal unity and improve the standard of living.

## HISTORY OF CITY AND SMART CITY

The genealogy of smart city has been in existence far back 1990s when developed countries started investing and included information communication technology (ICT) into the modern construction and infrastructures. Alawadhi et al. (2012) reported that the first institute of smart city was the California Institute which discussed and targeted how major cities can be designed to integrate information technologies (IT). The concept of smart city is based on how a community can be digitised to reflect computer development and yet there has not been an agreed definition.

New innovations on ICTs have positively influenced cities by obtaining sustainable and efficient systems. The innovations have been mostly embraced by the end-user or people in the communities thereby developing cities into smart cities. Far back in Van Basterlaer literature in 1998, the context of smart city was used and the meaning was not clear as sourced from Anthopoulos and Fitsilis (2013). However, the term smart city was coined in late twentieth century and rooted to accommodate ICT and developed for cities by the construction sector. Although smart city became more popular along the way and it recently gained more adoption in 2005 by a number of technology companies for the purpose of incorporating it into urban infrastructures and services to complex information system to promote good operations within the urban areas or cities (Cisco, 2005; IBM, 2009; Siemens, 2004). Other scholars see it as a vision to integrate ICTs in a secured manner to assess the quality of a city; these qualities include infrastructural facilities and services like buildings (schools, libraries, hospitals, commercial buildings, mass housing, etc.), electrical invention, water and road network, transportation, public safety plant, law enforcement, waste management, etc. In addition, smart city is a means of forming a new innovation technological enhancement in the planning, advancement and function of cities.

## DEFINITION OF CITY AND SMART CITY

Increase in population tends to increase the settlement of people in the urban spaces over time. This is as a result of countless benefits in the cities or urban areas. City has been described as a potential driver of economy, social and environmental activities that influence the development of people settlement and their communities. Cities are also defined as a place or location or metropolis where different people come together to form settlement, different beliefs, different culture and different behaviour that is stronger with negative consequential effects if not properly managed.

Generally, smart as a word has been used in various research works, context, programme and sectors, such words includes smart people, smart industry, smart cities, smart government, smart communities and smart education (Giffinger et al., 2007). However, when talking about 'smart', there is something paramount which is ICT in every area or sector. Giffinger et al. (2007) continued in his research to define smart city as an urban settlement that was designed in order to incorporate new technologies in regular basis with proper monitoring of all the digitised designed features. Smart city cut across modern transportation technologies that improve mobility of residents in the city, security, energy conservation, sustainable development and green structures, etc.

Further definitions described smart city as a logic developed within the activities of all city's infrastructures and services. While others stated its definition in relation to creating an environment that is suitable and attractive to many generations of its inhabitants.

Finally, smart cities serve as a spotlight resource preservation and management in order to meet the rising need of people and their communities. It improves and encourages new methods of schemes in cities since the city can be monitored through automated systems. When adequate data are collected digitally, cities can provide insights, innovations and varying opportunities that can prosper a quality life and also improve the living condition of the environment.

## CONSTRUCTION INDUSTRY AND SMART CITIES

There have been various views on what a smart city is in time pass, the new innovation however has been induced to many sectors like the construction industry, oil and gas, education or institution, health, etc. Lack of unified consensus on this emerging term has led to confusion among many sectors. It has also brought confusion among urban policy-makers as they are making frantic effort in enacting policies that would make their cities smart (Albino & Dangelico, 2015).

Construction is a vital sector in nation building. Relating construction to smart city has helped in generating, distributing and consumption of energy within buildings and infrastructures, consumption of raw materials with the use of IT, management of materials and other available resources through creation of mass housing for affordable price and improved standard of living within the urban centres. Creating a sustainable environment through smart supply and disposing system has encouraged an ideal environment, technological development and networking, easy access to transportation (road, air and water) or mobility, buildings and infrastructures (health centre, market, water, business, etc.) and all other social amenities or facilities.

A good communication network and active monitoring system on services rendered by government and people will have a positive effect on the invention of smart cities. Improvement and the use of ICTs (installing CCTV cameras within the buildings and infrastructures) will help reduce crime and increase security within the economy and the environment.

## CHARACTERISTICS OF SMART CITIES

Smart city is described as such that has the six major performing arms that an environment or a geographic location can be summarised with. The completeness of a succinct definition of smart city must reflect the calibres of people domiciled in the area, the prevailing economy, people-oriented governance, and technologically oriented mobility and geographical environment and the standard of living of the people are the major performing arms identified by Giffinger et al. (2007). These aims or characteristics emanate from smart combinations of endowment and decisive operations coupled with awareness of the citizen in the community or city. The six parts identified by Giffinger et al. (2007) are outcome of findings but the pattern and hierarchy are not conclusive.

The performance indicator of a smart city is a function of three variables. These variables are illustrated in Fig. 2.1.

### Economy

Government is a very important element in nation building; anything that needs establishment has to pass through the approval of the government and follow the policies and laws of the nation. Smart governance encourages modification in government, coordination and planning processes with private and public participation. Implementation of construction projects has a large percentage in the economy development and quality production by

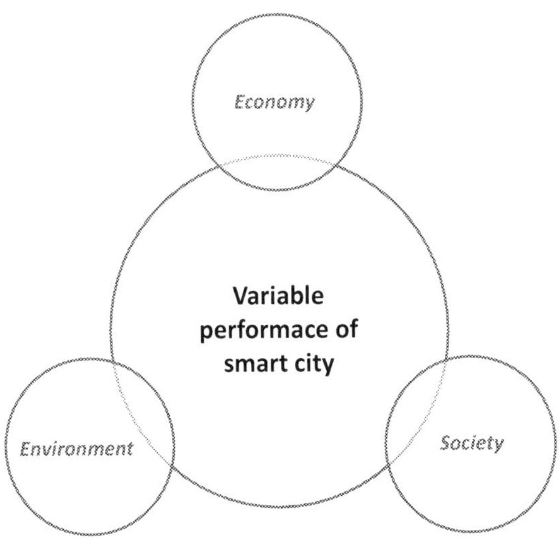


**Fig. 2.1. Performing Variables Indicator of a Smart City.**

the administration. It helps to develop collaboration with different economy sectors, private and public organisation units, and promote business and production of goods and services in the communities, quality research work and their usage through the help of ICTs. This is widely used from available public digital data to enable the involvement of people, end-users and members of the communities to partake in the public decision-making process, and also the participation of local authorities coupled with the involvement of the people within the community or urban area. Finally, the growth of the economy is the involvement of people, private and public sector or organisation and government.

### Environment

The environment we live has a great influence on our day-to-day activities as human beings. A conducive environment will enhance productivity and encourage a flexible way of life. Smart cities are actively in support of a better environment for people and their communities by creating more institutions for learning and carrying out research work, construction and connection of land, air and water movement, promoting business, generating and distributing energy, development in the use of ICTs, mass housing, convenient environment, waste management, use of available natural resources, etc.

### Society

Culture, beliefs, norms, rules and regulations, policy, health, government, social issues are important aspects in developing a smart city. The innovation of smart city is basically more of the technical but also socialisation since the participation of every individual or person in the environment is also essential and the needs of the society must be taking into account. In achieving a smart life, civil societies in the city, local government authorities, the elders, leaders and rulers must come together and focus on the safety of the people, their cultures and ethnic values, health, education, mobility and easy access within and outside the environment, relaxation centres, business growth and training and social unity.

## SMART CITY FRAMEWORKS

The concepts and ways en route for a city to becoming smart are as diverse as cities themselves. Literatures have revealed that cities are recorded for close to three quarters of greenhouse gases effects. Worldwide networking of labour forces, institutions and information all have their repercussions on cities. Smart ideas require that measures taken should serve different purposes such as aesthetics, social, economic, spatial and structural consideration.

The use of urban informatics and technologies to improve effective and efficiency of services rendered will help the growth of a city to become smart. Some of these approaches are technology-oriented while others put aspect like the social foremost. The application of these approaches will aim to stop challenges faced by an ordinary city as they drive towards improving efforts, resources and satisfaction. This is thus expressed as many out of the numerous goals of establishing a smart city. However, the gain of new technologies must be greatly utilised for public interest and also preserve creative freedom in public spaces. These are achievable through smart ideas whose implementation requires active public participations.

At the strategic level of a city becoming smart, its ideas should be built on sustainability and flexibility because cities systems are not rigid but are susceptible to influences. A better understanding of the concept paramount is analysing the subject in these three theoretical frameworks. These are technology, human and institutional frameworks.

## Technology Framework

One of the most important aspects of smart cities is the use of technology. When a city is technologically stable, there are combinations of different technological infrastructures, that is, virtual city, information city, intelligent city, digital city and ubiquitous city. This is solely for the purpose of connecting the community through up-to-date communication infrastructures, such as cyberspace, flexible service-oriented computing infrastructures making it easier to be connected to available network and creating innovativeness and standard of living for the people and their environment. Also, it is driven to meet the needs of government in various sectors and improve the growth of the economy by creating job opportunities, electricity, power, water, etc.

## Human Framework

Human framework is related to the people living within the cities, that is, the end-users, the needs of the people is basically on the social, economy and environment. Providing a sustainable environment by improving the infrastructures and creating jobs for the people is another dimension use in developing a smart city. This involves providing social infrastructures (health, education, training, business, culture and arts, commerce, etc.) in order to build skilled workforce to enhance competitiveness in the global knowledge economy and eventually exploiting these human potentials to promote knowledge economy and innovation processes.

### Institutional Framework

Smart city is a strategic means to broaden the use of IT and the residents of the city with the help of relevant authorities (different institutions and government officials). There is a deal to enhance and improve the use of IT in order to improve daily life quality. A smart city initiative is a conscious technological catalyst employed to solve social and business challenges within the city. The involvement of institutions is a very important success to smart city innovation.

Finally, the framework to smart cities are relevance to the skills of promoting the cities, as update should be made regularly on the use of IT, studying and research should be carried out by the institutions, humans should handle and manage properly the new tools or utensils for their benefits and environment and be security alert. These frameworks should be a synergy of developing a city into smart city so that the objectives of the innovation can be reached using available resources with caution and providing a sustainable environment worth living for everyone.

## FEATURES OF SMART CITY

The developments and changes made in urban centres are attributing to a progressive and efficient resources environment and these are having influences on the quality of living. Generally speaking, some features of smart cities are as follow:

1. They incorporate, generate and distribute new energy.
2. They encourage new social and technological innovation linking to existing infrastructures.
3. They help control traffic and transportation, movement of human, goods and services.
4. They focus on a productive governance and public participation.
5. They promote the use of available resources.
6. They create easy environment for people.

7. Smart cities make use of ITs to effectively and efficiently use of physical infrastructures through data analysis and artificial intelligence to support a strong and healthy economy.
8. Smart cities involve the people within the community to make decision for the development of their local government.
9. The use of open innovation processes and e-participation.
10. They promote unity within the community and their environment.
11. They encourage economy growth between two or more countries.
12. They improve the collective intelligence of institutions through e-governance.
13. With regard to bringing intellectually expected changes in a city, smart cities bring about the concept of learning and relearning, adaptation, with effective swift response to identified practice.
14. They are scientifically planned cities that give high standard of living.
15. Smart cities encourage mass housing; therefore making good shelter available for everyone on their own.
16. Hazardous activities are prevented in smart cities.
17. Also, there is reduction in crime and increase in security through the help of ICT-enabled systems.

## CONCLUSION

A city is meant to always move from a state to a better one especially in development and services offered to the residents. But for this to be fully visible to everyone involved, frameworks and features embedded into the smart city system have to be made simple enough in order to increase awareness. This part is a very important aspect of everything concerned with the transformation from a normally advanced city to better and more sustainable ones. The benefits to be incurred from raising awareness about the smart city system will channel the rate at development and overall improvement in the economy of the society. The full adoption of this practice will not only enhance the activities of the construction industry; it will also bring a general upsurge in relativeness to services provided which will propel greater opportunities that the city can tap from so as to move from a perceived redundancy to an improved state.

## REFERENCES

Alawadhi, S., Aldama-Nalda, A., Chourabi, H., Gil-Garcia, J. R., Leung, S., Mellouli, S., ... Walker, S. (2012). Building understanding of Smart City Initiatives. *International Conference on Electronic Government*, *7443*, 40–53.

Albino, V., & Dangelico, R. M. (2015). Smart cities: Definitions, dimensions, performance, and initiatives. *Journal of Urban Technology*, *22*(1), 3–21. doi: 10.1080/10630732.2014.942092

Anthopoulos, L., & Fitsilis, P. (2013). Using classification and road mapping techniques for smart city viability's realization. *Electronic Journal of e-Government*, *11*(1), 326–336.

Cisco. (2005). Dubai: The Smart City. Retrieved from http://www.cisco.com/web/learning/le34/downloads/689/nobel/2005/docs/Abdulhakim_Malik.pdf

Giffinger, R., Fertner, C., Kramar, H., Kalasek, R., Pichler-Milanovi, N., & Meijers, E. (2007). *Smart Cities: Ranking of European Medium-Sized Cities.* Vienna: Centre of Regional Science (SRF), Vienna University of Technology. Retrieved from http://www.smartcities.eu/download/smart_cities_final_report.pdf

IBM. (2009). IBM Offers Smarter City assessment tool to help cities. Prepare for challenges and opportunities of unprecedented urbanization. Retrieved from https://www-03.ibm.com/press/us/en/pressrelease/27791

Mori, K., & Christodoulou, A. (2012). Review of sustainability indices and indicators: Towards a New City Sustainability Index (CSI). *Environmental Impact Assessment Review*, *32*(1), 94–106. doi:10.1016/j.eiar.2011.06.001

Siemens. (2004). Stadt der Zukunft. Retrieved from http://www.siemens.com/innovation/de/publikationen/zeitschriften_pic_future/PoF_Fruehjahr_2004/SmartCity.htm

United Nations. (2016). The sustainable development goals report. Retrieved from https://www.un.org/development/desa/publications/the-sustainable-developmentgoals-report-2016.html

# 3

# THE SMART CITY PROCESS


## ABSTRACT

*The smart city process encompasses many features. The two chapters before this has succinctly introduced the concepts and some parts that relate to smart city. The process in implementation is dissected in this section of the book. It starts from the conceptualisation of the process to further definitions of the subject. Also, traits attributed to smart cities are explained in smart environment, economy, governance, living, people and mobility. Urbanisation brings along with it several features and terminologies. One of which is smartisation fused into the smart city process. The smartisation of the city system aim to bring developments in making the city wireless and developing smart families at the same time. Also, there are smart general administrations and improvement of social administrations, development of smart transportation, improvement of smart medicinal treatment, development of smart city administration, development of green city, and development of smart vacationer focus. Other smart city processes include the drivers, barriers, and benefits.*



**Keywords:** Digital city; Smart city conceptualisation; Smart city drivers; Smart city framework; sustainability; sustainable development


## INTRODUCTION

Urbanisation is expanding as more individuals move towards cities (United Nations, 2014). As a result of this, most cities on the planet are faced with challenges of assets over-use, deficient administrations and high rate of ecological contamination (Bifulco, Tregua, Amitrano, & D'Auria, 2015). Thus, cities are currently making colossal moves to accomplish a more reasonable advancement taking tripods of sustainability (economic, environmental and social) into thought (Toli & Murtagh, 2020). In the wake of this, the innovation integration that offers a greater quality life to its partners in every aspect of the metropolitan condition is named the smartisation process (Bifulco et al., 2015).

The smart city started its development in the 1970s when urban settings embraced an advanced setup that concentrated on advances and non-material structures installed in the physical space of the city (Ishida & Isbister, 2000). In 2014, 53% of the worldwide populace lived in cities and it is normal that this number will develop to 66% by 2050 (United Nations, 2014). Accordingly, pioneers must outline new methodologies to upgrade city execution and sustainability (Ben Letaifa, 2015). Many examinations rank city areas as indicated by social, financial and environmental criteria and depict well-performing urban communities. Nonetheless, few authors handle how to change these urban communities and pioneers' methodology for such change (McKinsey & Company, 2013).

Since the city has assorted settings, sizes and assets, a need exists for an all encompassing and comprehensive structure that conceptualises diverse parts of the brilliant city and discloses the vital strides to take after, the system ought to incorporate a few building hinders in one `IT-based advancement urban biological community'. In reality, keen advancements change smart areas' open and private administrations by coordinating constant interchanges, subjects' needs and data, and by upgrading reasonableness (Oxford Economics, 2011). The need to adjust social advancement and monetary development in a setting of high urbanisation is the principal driver of the overall enthusiasm for keen urban areas (Vanolo, 2013).

In a report by (Giffinger et al., 2007) where it is stated that the European cities think that it is hard to combine sustainable development in urban settings with its aggressiveness. By and by, the government needs to investigate policies that will advance city sustainability and also its execution (Ben Letaifa, 2015). In any case, the dangers in smart city arrangement have expanded the journey for superior quality administrations which had driven most cities to begin the process of smartisation, a way that gives a superior personal satisfaction to its inhabitants utilising integration of innovation (Bifulco et al., 2015).

Moreover, urbanisation had been on the high side as individuals tend to move to urban areas for a superior green field, in this way causing clog, contamination, wastage and social annihilation (European Commission, 2013).

Besides, numerous researchers, be that as it may, see the city as an aggregate substance, reflecting a solitary homogenous body with one voice (Vanolo, 2013). Regardless of developing premium, the administration and promoting writing for all intents and purposes overlooks the procedure of strategising smart city areas (Ben Letaifa, 2015).

More so, the difficulties in smart city areas have fuelled the scan for better quality administrations and have driven city areas to start the process of smartisation, a way towards the coordination of innovation in each part of the urban condition to offer a superior personal satisfaction to its partners (Bifulco, Tregua, Amitrano, & D'Auria, 2016). Recently, consideration on sustainability as the objective for smartisation, and on information communication technology (ICT) (data and interchanges innovation or advancements) as a pertinent instrument or as the way to tend to smart procedures, particularly given the discoveries contained in official reports discharged by associations and nearby organisations (Meijer & Rodrigyez-Bolivar, 2015).

## THE CONCEPTUALISATION OF SMART CITIES

As of late, the conceptualisation of a smart city has created an extensive number of concentrates from researchers, tertiary establishments and construction sectors associated with smart tasks (Nam & Pardo, 2011a). ICTs are presently vigorously associated with the administration and management of city areas, where they are utilised as instruments and as assets to enhance personal satisfaction, accomplish reasonable advancement, and make a more open and inventive urban setting through the investment of a few performing artists (Anthopoulos & Tougountzoglou, 2012).

The incorporation of new viewpoints conveyed to consider extraordinary and creative factors in administration and administration of the urban territories, and this procedure turned the attention on more unpredictable conceptualisations. For example, the smart city in which human and social capital and customary and present-day correspondence foundations are joined to bear on the sustainable monetary development and a higher personal satisfaction through an appropriate administration of accessible assets (Caragliu, Del Bo & Nijkamp, 2011; Schaffers et al., 2011).

Several phrasings have been utilised in different literatures by various authors, for example, creative, information, intelligent, ubiquitous, wired, hybrid, digital, learning, humane, knowledge and smart have all been used in many articles (Nam & Pardo, 2011a). Among all these, setting over the most broadly utilised term is the smart city or digital city. In opposition, some researches do not underpin the definitions above as just global ventures that shared the prospect of practical city and depict the development of smart city (Shen, Jorge Ochoa, Shah, & Zhang, 2011; Tregua, D'Auria, & Bifulco, 2015). It is stated that a smart city is a moderately new idea that is exceedingly setting subordinate (nation, government, characteristic assets, information technology (IT) learning and limits) (Weisi & Ping, 2014). Although any cities with smart industries that consolidate ICT in its framework, present-day transportation innovations and has smart tenants is said to be a smart city (Giffinger et al., 2007). It is therefore important to note that the line between smart cities communities and comparable ideas, for example, inventive and smart urban areas is foggy, and numerous pioneers guarantee their cities are smart without meeting a specific standard (Hollands, 2008). Most articles concerning smart city communities concentrate on interests in particular advancement territories that prompt sustainable development and better nature of life (Dawes & Pardo, 2002).

Smart communities are the consequence of a thick advancement biological system that incorporates far-reaching social communications and taught work that creates an incentive through data utilised. Smart city administration is more mind-boggling than conventional city administration. While customary city administration is about urban arranging, smart administration suggests coordination among a few partners collaborating in various subsystems (transportation, health, education, condition, etc.) inside a solitary city large-scale framework that incorporates full utilisation of ICT with the city's assets and neighbourhood attributes (Weisi & Ping, 2014).

Most smart city initiatory rotated round the smartisation of existing urban communities. Thus far, the New Songdo city is the main smart city on the planet which is assembled not because of smartisation. It is the greatest land private property wander ever recorded in the history (Woyke, 2009). The New Songdo city is worked as ubiquitous city where all gadgets and administrations are connected to a remote data (Chohan, 2014). In this manner, the specialised design of smart city is application layer, arrange layer and discernment layer. The term smart city went for acquiring information innovation all frameworks to the future age and through internet arrived at 'Internet of Things'. Henceforth, 'Smart Planet = Internet + Internet of Things' (Yongmin, 2010).

## SMART CITY DEFINITIONS

Diverse words have been utilised as a part of the literature, for example, smart, learning, humane, innovative, information, knowledge, wired, digital, hybrid, ubiquitous and insightful to give a point by point outlines utilised inside the local settings (Nam & Pardo, 2011a). 'Smart city' and 'digital city' are generally utilised, lamentably, most analysts do not bolster the two portrayal's definition, as supranational foundation ventures presents sustainable city as the augmentation of the idea of smart city (Shen et al., 2011; Tregua et al., 2015).

Toli and Murtagh (2020) characterises a smart city as one that utilises data and interchanges innovation (ICT) to upgrade its bearableness, workability and manageability. The committee recognises gather, correspondence and mash as the three centre elements of a smart city. A smart city gathers data about itself through sensors, different devises and existing frameworks; it imparts that information utilising wired or remote systems and crunches (examines) that information to comprehend what is occurring now and what is probably going to occur next. The most well-known definition of smart city is stated below.

Caragliu et al. (2011) described smart city according to a belief that a city is said to be smart when there is a cordial and relatable relationships between components (human and social capital) with the aid of digitalised tools targeted at creating an enhanced economy channelled towards improving whole life cycle of the building, structures and the quality of life all at once in respect to proper governance and effective resources management policies.

Likewise, Schaffers et al. (2011), another researcher viewed smart city as a concept driven towards sustainability due to emergence of factors expressed in technologies, demands, value creations and managements. With the view to creating a better interaction and value for cost and improved general interface between man and his environment, a smart city concept is agreed effective in bridging the gap between sustainability defined now and the one to be expressed in realities of tomorrow.

## TRAITS OF SMART CITY AREAS

In expressing the traits embedded in smart city areas, Giffinger et al. (2007) highlighted six most-normal pointers of brilliant smart areas, they are smart environment, smart economy, smart governance, smart living, smart people and smart mobility. These traits are explained below.

### Smart Environment

City pioneers may investigate openings in building stock and vitality administration range. The utilisation of creative innovations, for example, sun power vitality and other inexhaustible wellsprings of power, can likewise upgrade the common habitat (Colldahl, Frey, & Kelemen, 2013). The smart environment has been examined regarding contamination reduction, natural asset administration, and the insurance and preservation of common living spaces through the productive utilisation of assets and also the re-utilise or substitution of normal assets to achieve sustainability objectives (Tanguary, Rajaonson, Lefebvre, & Lanoie, 2010).

## Smart Economy

The smart economy bunches all highlights identified with financial intensity, for example, business, advancement, efficiency and adaptability of the work showcase, as well as the worldwide extension of the neighbourhood economy. The advancement of a smart city is firmly connected to the production of an urban setting that empowers new modern exercises (Bronstein, 2009).

## Smart Governance

Smart governance concerns natives' support in urban basic leadership forms, the co-formation of new administrations for an enhanced personal satisfaction, and the usage of various instruments for coordinated effort, benefit reconciliation and information trade (Bélissent, 2010; Kolsaker & Lee-Kelley, 2013; Bifulco, Tregua, Amitrano, & D'Auria, 2016). E-administrations, for example, e-government, online networking and group sourcing incorporate all gathering in straightforward basic leadership forms prompting smart governance (Ben Letaifa, 2015).

## Smart Living

This includes enhancing life quality regarding administrations, improving engaging quality for vacationers, and advancing social attachment and wellbeing. Smart living incorporates social offices, e-wellbeing, social administrations and open security devices, for example, reconnaissance frameworks and between crises benefits systems (Toppeta, 2010). Smart living has been related to personal satisfaction, to be specific, lodging, culture, health, tourism and a particular enthusiasm for the scan for large amounts of social attachment (Bifulco et al., 2016).

## Smart People

Smart people are the outcome of ethnic and social decent variety, resistance, innovativeness and engagement. Cities may offer online courses and workshops, online help with instruction, and projects and administrations custom-made to raise social capital and capacity (Toppeta, 2010). Moreover, smart people are characterised through the nature of social communications in urban areas, receptiveness towards various societies, the advancement of human capital, the training of individuals, and the part of ICT in the change of support and the lessening of the computerised partition (Giffinger et al., 2007).

### Smart Mobility

Urban arranging is the most ideal approach to accomplish smart mobility. Urban arranging moves the concentration from individual to aggregate methods of transportation through the broad utilisation of data and correspondences innovations (ICT) (Ben Letaifa, 2015). Smart mobility centres both around sustainable and bury modular transport frameworks offering sheltered and secure conditions using ICT and on nearby, national and global availabilities (Bifulco, Amitrano, & Tregua, 2014).

## THE SMARTISATION PROCESS OF A CITY

The approach towards smart urban territories has progressed through an accentuation on no less than one parts supporting the smartisation process. Regardless, simply compromising most of the spaces of intercession in perspective of the dedication of ICT can help urban regions to finish continuing and viable money related improvement and a predominant individual fulfilment for urban accomplices (Anthopoulos & Tougountzoglou, 2012). This process of joining assorted smart exercises in urban and metropolitan settings has been refined through the undertakings of different accomplices (Tregua et al., 2015). The endeavour to consider smart urban groups have provoked the generation of models which assemble the estimations of urban life to be overhauled and made through the use of keen city wanders (Bifulco et al., 2016). The Center of Regional Science at the Vienna University of Technology attempt to influence a smart city to show, which, beginning today, remains the most referred to and most frequently used (Schaffers et al., 2011). Besides, ICT is believed to be a key segment with specific qualities: it is regardless of what you look like at its drivers, particularly, a key enabling specialist for urban groups to address these challenges in a splendid manner (Bifulco et al., 2016).

## THE CONTENT OF SMARTISATION PROCESS

Smart city will be the future trend of city development as summarised in Table 3.1 and coded in the Fig. 3.1. The procedure of smart city can be arranged into three interesting parts, including the development of the general framework, the development of the open platform and the development of utilisation frameworks. Among every one of these levels, the development of used framework has gotten extraordinary thoughts around the world. However, resistance and open security applications have been connected to various zones of smart city, being developed of digital city or wireless city, development of smart family, smart general administrations and improvement of social administration, development of smart transportation, improvement of smart medicinal treatment, development of smart city administration, and development of green city and smart vacationer focus (Kehua, Jie, & Hongbo, 2011).

### Development of Wireless City

Wireless expansive system, Wi-Fi innovation, web and Wi-MAX can be based on the premise of solid fibre optics network and these will cover the entire city. These can give many elements of urban administration and service frameworks for the environment, guests, open and private organisations. The capacities may incorporate crisis in broadcasting communications, versatile dispatching of crisis criticism, portable video conferencing and versatile wireless video reconnaissance (Zhiping, 2008).

### Development of Smart Family

Sensor contraption can be added to the internet to arrive at the Internet of Things. In this way, everything can be viewed as terminal and system brought

**Table 3.1. Content of Smartisation Process.**

| Code | Meaning |
|---|---|
| DWC | Development of wireless city |
| DMF | Development of smart family |
| SAIA | Smart general administrations and improvement of social administration |
| DST | Development of smart transportation |
| ISMT | Improvement of smart medicinal treatment |
| DSMA | Development of smart city administration |
| DGC | Development of green city |
| DSVF | Development smart vacationer focus |

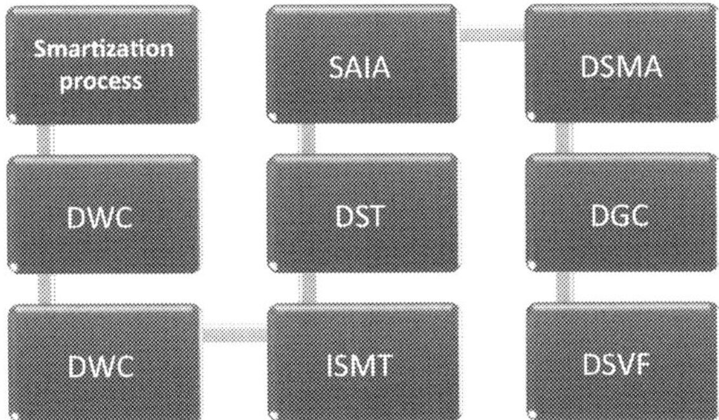


**Fig. 3.1. Content of Smartisation Process.**

to accomplish the incorporated and remote control for both electrical and mechanical services. For instant, the lighting and other electrical gadgets, even entryways can be accomplished utilising intelligent control which is a vital advantage of information innovation to a smart city (Kehua et al., 2011).

### Smart General Administrations and Improvement of Social Administration

Social service framework can be set to manage gripes of individuals, ask for help and personnel administration which involves the keen management of the whole city. On this ground, fundamental platform administrations for metropolitan arranging and reaction and public management are given to improve the legislature. The government would then be able to evaluate and examine the genuine information gathered in an urban district and gives a more strike and better services to the group (Kortuem, Kawsar, Fitton, & Sundramoorthy, 2010).

### Development of Smart Transportation

The demands and traffic nature in the most city has made the Internet of Things, sensor network and other innovation to change the customary transportation to the smart movement administration technique, for example, utilising programmed movement, light control framework, movement control strategies in urban settings, etc. (Kehua et al., 2011).

### Improvement of Smart Medicinal Treatment

The Internet of Things can help the medical focusses to achieve an astute medicinal administration of materials and smart therapeutic care, likewise help the electronic accumulation, breaking down, storage, exchanging and sharing of therapeutic details of interest about each other and data inside the interior medicinal organisations. Similarly, the requirements of smart administration, therapeutic details of interest checking and the supply of medicinal hardware can be met (Qui, 2010).

### Development of Smart City Administration

Because of the ever-display network, the future city on the cutting edge can make utilisation of both the 3G and 4G remote networks. Through the private network, information can be exchanged, chipped away at and used to build up the major city administration style to accomplish a smooth management (Krassimira, 2009). The urban framework and administration can be accomplished utilising smart city management (Kehua et al., 2011).

### Development of Green City

The interoperability of various frameworks and systems administration constituted by different gadgets and influencing the most favourable position to the utilisation of this asset of following and caution to build up the most recent metropolitan model and arrangement of the green city can be accomplished inside the breaking points of a city. Moreover, data gathering and transmission, stockpiling with its show, and in addition sound and video control and caution can likewise be accomplished utilising this technological platform (Kehua et al., 2011).

### Development Smart Vacationer Focus

The particular technique for passing on data is through smart visitor focus. In light of the first visitor focus information and the Internet of Things, the administration of undertaking-related vacationer focus, for example, client connection administration, operational district administration, local improvement and tourism market abroad, smart administration of tracking, social occasion of tourism data and anticipating advancement can be accomplished (Kehua et al., 2011).

## SUSTAINABILITY AND ICT IN SMART CITIES

The expanding number of smart city activities can be connected to the dispersion and combination of new innovations, specifically, ICTs and information administration functionalities, extended from rudimentary information obtaining to information preparing and elucidation. These advances have been broadly abused because of the dissemination of cell phones, which enable individuals to take an interest in and add to their urban and metropolitan conditions (Kirwan, 2015).

The critical pretended by individuals, the alleged human segment, inside the smartisation process has prompted an alternate conceptualisation of advances as clever instruments went for the production of urban communities with an enhanced personal satisfaction and at the change of human investment through administrations co-creation (Kirwan, 2015; Nam & Pardo, 2011a, 2011b). A smart city must send smart figuring advances consolidating the utilisation of programming frameworks, server foundations, organise foundations and customer gadgets to associate diverse urban administrations and partners (Akesson, Skalen, & Edvardsson, 2008).

Probably the most created ICT applications in smart cities areas are GPS advancements to upgrade transportation and movement stream; database advances in wellbeing, vitality proficiency and instruction; design acknowledgement programming to enhance security frameworks; and versatile advances to connect with individuals in administrations co-creation or social activities also, at the change of human cooperation through administrations co-creation (Bulu, 2009; Kirwan, 2015). The innovative components required to send smart activities incorporate the execution of the fundamental equipment (sensors, remote gear, etc.) and programming (manmade brainpower, master frameworks, etc.) to make a 'physical-computerised condition of brilliant cities' (Li, Li, & Li, 2015; Schaffers et al., 2011).

Toli and Murtagh (2020) identify collect, communication and crunch as the key attributes of a smart city. The sustainability, workability and livelihood of smart cities are enhanced through ICT. Therefore, a smart city is one that has adequate knowledge about itself has the capacity of making its occupants aware of its impact. The idea of sustainability is broadly perceived as bringing tomorrow's realities into realisation today without neglect to situations presented at the moment (World Commission on Environment and Development (WCED), 1987). Meijer and Rodrigyez-Bolivar (2015) affirmed that the goal of any smartisation is sustainability while ICTs are the keys to smart city processes. Therefore, Bifulco et al. (2015) regard ICT and sustainability as the board parts for smart projects.

## SMART CITIES DRIVERS

Toli and Murtagh (2020) identified inadequate infrastructure, growing stress, growing urbanisation, growing environmental challenges, growing economics competition, growing expectations and rapidly improving technology capabilities as the key drivers of smart cities.

### Inadequate Infrastructure

Urbanisation is putting a critical strain on city frameworks that were, as a rule, worked for populaces a small amount of their present size. A significant part of the created world has a framework that is close or past its plan life, requiring monstrous updates. For example, in 2013, the American Society of Civil Engineers gave the United States a general review of D+ for its framework. In the interim, a great part of the creating scene has an absent or insufficient framework, requiring monstrous form outs.

### Growing Stress

The present urban cities confront huge difficulties in expanding populaces, ecological and administrative prerequisites, declining charge bases and spending plans and expanded expenses in the meantime many are encountering troublesome developing agonies extending from contamination, swarming and sprawl to lacking lodging, high joblessness and rising wrongdoing rates.

### Growing Urbanisation

Urban areas convey many advantages, more noteworthy work openings, more noteworthy access to social insurance and instruction, and more prominent access to amusement, culture and human expressions (Vlahov & Galea, 2002). Thus, individuals are moving to urban areas at an exceptional rate. More than 700 million individuals will be added to urban populaces throughout the following 10 years. The United Nations (UN) extends that the world's urban communities should suit an extra 3 billion occupants by the centre of the century. A current UN report recommends that 40,000 new urban areas will be required around the world.

### Growing Environmental Challenges

Urban areas house half of the total populace, however, utilise 66% of the world's vitality and produce three fourths of the world's carbon dioxide discharges. On the off chance that we will relieve environmental change, it should occur in urban areas. Numerous districts and urban areas have forceful the atmosphere and ecological objectives – objectives that cannot become without the assistance of keen advancements.

### Growing Economics Competition

The world has seen a quick ascent in the rivalry between urban communities to secure the ventures, employment, organisations and ability for financial achievement. Progressively, the two organisations and people assess a city's 'innovation remainder' in choosing where to find.

### Growing Expectations

Cities are progressively getting a moment, anyplace, whenever, customised access to data and administrations through cell phones and computers. Furthermore, they progressively expect that same sort of access to city administrations. Truth be told, a 2013 UN review of more than 560,000 residents from 194 nations uncovered their best needs are a decent instruction, better social insurance and a fair and responsive government (Assembly, 2006). We additionally realise that individuals need to live in urban areas that can give proficient transportation, high-data transmission interchanges and solid employment markets.

### Rapidly Improving Technology Capabilities

Huge numbers of the smart city drivers recorded above are negatives issues that request arrangements. There are certain drivers too, particularly the quick advance in innovation. The expenses of gathering, imparting and crunching information have dove. Furthermore, a significant part of the required innovation is as of now set up.

## SMART CITY BARRIERS

Regardless of the intense drivers in support, the way to smart city has deterrents en route as explained by Smart Cities Council (2013):

## Lack of a Smart City Visionary

Each parade needs a pioneer. Now and then that authority originates from a chosen official, a leader or board individual who goes about as the smart city champion. Smart city authority can likewise originate from somewhere else in the organisation, a city administrator or an arranging executive. On the other hand, it can originate from outside city corridor by and large with contribution from business pioneers, metro associations or open private organisations.

## Lack of Citizen Engagement

Smart city development is frequently kept down by an absence of lucidity about what a smart city is and how it can improve the situation subjects. Accordingly, numerous partners are unconscious of the smart city choices that have discovered achievement as of now. Frequently, there is a correspondences issue. Urban areas ought to be careful about being excessively unique with their smart city activities, perceive that natives think about administrations that improve their lives, and change their engagement as per their needs. Urban areas need to create a balanced interaction between what the residents require and the business environment because capturing the minds of the residents is essential towards creating things to purchase. They took off savvy meters without clarifying how clients would profit. They endured customer backfire and the rest went down the drain.

## Lack of Integrated Services

To the degree cities connected ICT previously, they connected it to their inside, siloed operations. The outcome has been a snatch sack of maturing applications that exclusive city workers can utilise. In spite of the fact this was a worthy practice in the most recent century, today we can and should permit resident access and self-benefit. There is no reason that nationals who need, for example, to open an eatery ought to need to make various applications to numerous city offices. In a brilliant city, a solitary entryway can accumulate every one of the information and package it out to the proper divisions. In like manner, occupants ought to have moment access to up-to-the-minute data about their vitality and water use, their assessments and charges, their social administrations projects and the sky is the limit from there. Furthermore, thoughts like Open Data not just enhance straightforwardness; they implement a human first point of view that is basic in keen urban areas.

## Lack of ICT Know-how

Despite the fact that industry has grown profoundly complex ICT abilities, few city governments have the financial plan or the vision to push the best in class. Since savvy urban areas are basically the infusion of ICT into each period of operations, this absence of ICT aptitudes puts urban communities off guard. Luckily, an ever increasing number of utilisations are offered as an administration, that is, they are facilitated in the cloud (out on the Internet) where they approach gigantic processing power, for all intents and purposes boundless capacity and inventive programming. Another, in addition to, is that the brilliant city segment has built up a substantial framework of experienced worldwide, provincial and nearby experts and specialist co-ops who are collaborating with urban areas to send ICT arrangements.

## Lack of Finance

Expense incomes are contracting in numerous urban communities, making framework extends progressively hard to fund. Truth to be told, a few urban communities have been compelled to execute sombreness measures, for example, furloughing representatives one day a month or curtailing travel and optional costs. However in the event that those urban areas stay antiquated while others modernise, they will endure considerably more, since urban communities should now contend all around. Luckily, new monetary models are rising. What's more, instalment advancements like e-Procurement or electronic advantages can enable urban areas to decrease expenses and free up cash to put resources into foundation and different changes. Some of them require next to zero forthright capital from the city. Rather, the city 'leases' its answer as it goes. What's more, execution contracts and shared income models between the city and arrangement sellers furnish urban communities with appealing financing arrangements.

## Siloed, Piecemeal Implementations

Urban communities regularly handle challenges in a piecemeal manner, because of here and now budgetary requirements and long haul conventions that partition city capacities into isolated, 'siloed' offices with little association.

Thus, many activities are worked to take care of a solitary issue in a solitary office, making 'islands of mechanization' that copy costs while making it hard to share frameworks or information. Building a shrewd city requires a framework wide view and a coordinated approach. The terrible news: all-encompassing considering and collective work are hard. The uplifting news: done right, they can spare time and empower new administrations that were unrealistic in a secluded, siloed demonstrate. For example, a city office can definitely cut the improvement time for another application by re-utilising information and programming modules as of now made by different offices. A city water utility can definitely cut the cost of a correspondences arrange by utilising one effectively worked out for an electric utility. What's more, a city can now and again lessen general data innovation (IT) costs by as much as 25% just by executing an ace IT engineering and innovation guide. This is not to recommend that urban communities must fund and execute many speculations at one time. Truth be told, it is altogether fine in any case only maybe a couple ventures. What is basic is that these ventures all fall into a bigger, coordinated arrangement with the goal that city speculations are not excess.

## SMART CITIES BENEFITS

Smart Cities Council (2013) states the accompanying ideas as the centre benefits of smart cities.

### Enhanced Sustainability

This implies giving individuals access to the assets they require without bargaining the capacity of future ages to address their own issues. Manageability has been characterised as a technique for utilising an asset so it is not exhausted or forever harmed. At the point when the Council utilises the term, it alludes to the earth, as well as to monetary substances. Savvy urban communities empower the productive utilisation of common, human and financial assets and advance cost sparing in the midst of grimness, and they are cautious stewards of citizen dollars. It is not tied in with putting colossal entireties of cash into new framework, it is tied in with influencing foundation to accomplish progressively and last longer for less.

### Enhanced Liveability

This implies a superior personal satisfaction for city occupants. In the shrewd city, individuals approach an agreeable, spotless, drew in, sound and safe way of life. The absolute most exceptionally esteemed perspectives incorporate cheap vitality, advantageous mass travel, great schools, quicker crisis reactions, clean water and air, low wrongdoing and access to various diversion and social alternatives.

### Enhance Workability

This implies quickened financial advancement. Put another way, it implies more employments and better occupations and expanded nearby GDP. In the shrewd city, individuals approach the establishments of thriving – the essential foundation benefits that let them contend on the planet economy. Those administrations incorporate broadband network; perfect, dependable, modest vitality; instructive open doors; moderate lodging and business space; and proficient transportation.

## CONCLUSION

As urbanisation is expanding, more individuals tend to move towards cities for a superior green field. Smartisation is the process whereby existing cities are converted to smart cities. Sustainability and ICT are the core objectives of smartisation. Therefore, the goal of any smartisation is sustainability while ICT is taken to be the key to smart city process. Thus, the tripod of sustainability is economic, social and environmental. The conceptualisation of smart city has created an extensive number of concentrates from researchers. Any cities with smart businesses that consolidate ICT in its framework, present-day transportation innovations and has smart tenants is said to be a smart city. Above all, the smart city will be the future pattern of city development. The content of smartisation process, therefore, include the development of the wireless city, development of the smart family, smart general administrations and improvement of social administration, development of smart transportation, improvement of smart medicinal treatment, development of smart city administration, development of the green city and smart vacationer focus. It is important to note that sustainability, workability and livelihood of smart cities are enhanced through ICT and, as a result of this, a smart city is capable of making its occupants aware of its impacts.

## REFERENCES

Akesson, M., Skalen, P., & Edvardsson, B. (2008). E-government and service orientation: Gaps between theory and practice. *International Journal of Public Sector Management*, *21*(1), 74–92.

Anthopoulos, L., & Tougountzoglou, T. (2012). A viability model for digital cities: Economic and acceptability factors. *Web 2.0 Technologies and Democratic Governance*, *1*, 79–96. doi:10.1007/978-1-4614-1448-3_6

Assembly, G. (2006). Report of the Commissioner-General of the United Nations Relief and Works Agency for Palestine Refugees in the Near East, pp. 18–20.

Bélissent, J. (2010). *Getting clever about Smart Cities: New opportunities require new business models*. Cambridge, MA: Forrester Research.

Ben Letaifa, S. (2015). How to strategize smart cities: Revealing the smart model. *Journal of Business Research*, 1–6.

Bifulco, F., Amitrano, C. C., & Tregua, M. (2014). Driving smartization through intelligient transport. *Chinese Business Review*, *13*(4), 243–259.

Bifulco, F., Tregua, M., Amitrano, C. C., & D'Auria, A. (2015). ICT and sustainability in smart cities management. *International Journal of Public Sector Management*, *29*, 132–142.

Bifulco, F., Tregua, M., Amitrano, C. C., & D'Auria, A. (2016). ICT and sustainability in smart cities management. *International Journal of Public Sector Management*, *29*(2), 132–147.

Bronstein, Z. (2009). Industry and smart city. *Dissent*, *56*(3), 27–34.

Bulu, M. (2009, November). Upgrading a city via technology. *Technological Forecasting and Social Change*, *89*, 63–67.

Caragliu, A., Del Bo, C., & Nijkamp, P. (2011). Smart cities in Europe. *Journal of Urban Technology*, *18*, 65–82. doi:10.1080/10630732.2011.601117

Chohan, U. W. (2014). *The ubilquitous city – Songdo*. Montreal: McGill Uniuversity.

Colldahl, C., Frey, S., & Kelemen, J. (2013). *Smart cities: Strategic sustainable development for an urban world*. Karlskrona: Blekinge Institute of Technology.

Dawes, S., & Pardo, T. (2002). Building collaborative digital government systems. *Adavances in Digital Government*, *26*, 259–273.

European Commission. (2013). Quality of life in cities. European Cities: Perception survey in 79. European Cities. Retrieved from https://ec.europa.eu/regional_policy/activity/urban/audit/index_en.cfm. doi: 10.2776/79403

Giffinger, R., Fertner, C., Kramar, H., Kalasek, R., Pichler-Milanovi, N., & Meijers, E. (2007). *Smart cities: Ranking of European Medium-Sized Cities.*

Vienna: Centre of Regional Science (SRF), Vienna University of Technology. Retrieved from http://www.smartcities.eu/download/smart_cities_final_report.pdf

Hollands, R. (2008). Will the real smart city please stand up? *City*, *12*(3), 303–320.

Ishida, T., & Isbister, K. (2000). *Digital cities: technologies, experience and future perspectives*. New York, NY: Springer.

Kehua, S., Jie, L., & Hongbo, F. (2011). Smart city and the applications. *International conference* on *electronics communication and control*, *16*(1), 4–11. doi:10.1109/ICECC.2011.6066743

Kirwan, C. G. (2015). Defining the middle ground: A ccomprehensive approach to the planing, design and implementation of smart city operating systems. *Cross Cultural Design Methods, Practice and Impact*, *91*(80), 316–327.

Kolsaker, A., & Lee-Kelley, L. (2013). Citizens' attitudes towards e-Government and e-Governance: A UK study. *International Journal of Public Sector Management*, *21*(7), 723–738.

Kortuem, B., Kawsar, F., Fitton, D., & Sundramoorthy, V. (2010). Smart objects as building blocks for the internet of things. *Internet Computing*, *14*(1), 44–51.

Krassimira, A. P. (2009). Enabling the smart city: The progress of city e-Government in Europe. *International Journal of Innovation and Regional Development*, *1*(7), 405–422.

Li, Y., Li, Y., & Li, J. (2015). An application and management system of smart city. In L. Yang & M. Zhao (Eds.), *Proceedings international industrial informatics and copmuter engineering conference* (Vol. 12), Amsterdam (1626–1630).

McKinsey & Company. (2013). *How to make a city great*. McKinsey & Company's Cities Special Initiative. Retrieved from https://www.mckinsey.com/~/media/mckinsey/featured%20insights/urbanization/how%20to%20make%20a%20city%20great/how_to_make_a_city_great.ashx

Meijer, A., & Rodrigyez-Bolivar, M. P. (2015). Governing the smart city: A review of the literature on smart urban governance. *International Review of Administrative Science*, *2*(1), 117–132.

Nam, T., & Pardo, T. A. (2011). Smart city as urban innovation: Focusing on management policy, and context. In E. Estevez & M. Janssen (Eds.),

*Proceeding of the 5th international conference on theory and practice of electronic governance ACM*, New York, NY (pp. 185–194).

Nam, T., & Pardo, T. A. (2011). *Conceptualizing smart city with dimensions of technology, people. A* research conference: Digital government innovation in challenging times, College Park, MD (pp. 282–291). doi:10.1145/2037556.2037602

Oxford Economics. (2011). *The new digital economy: How it will transform business*. Oxford: Oxford Economics.

Qui, X. (2010). Smart Heathcare: Application of the internet of things in medical treatment and health. *Information Construction*, *5*, 56–58.

Schaffers, H., Komninos, N., Pallot, M., Trousse, B., Nilsson, M., & Olivera, A. (2011). Smart cities and the future internet: Towards cooperation frameworks for open innovation. *The Future Internet*, 66(56), 431–446.

Shen, L. Y., Jorge Ochoa, J., Shah, M. N., & Zhang, X. (2011). The application of urban sustainability indicators: A comparison between various practices. *Habitat International*, *35*(1), 17–29.

Smart Cities Council. (2013). *Smart cities readiness guide, the planning manual for building tomorrow cities*. Seattle, WA: Tahne Davis and Anne Schoenecker of Davis Design.

Toli, A. M., & Murtagh, N. (2020). The Concept of Sustainability in Smart City Definitions. *Frontiers in Built Environment*, 6(77), 1–15.

Toppeta, D. (2010). The smart city vision: How innovation and ICT can build smart, livable, sustainable cities. *Innovation Knowledge Found*, *5*, 1–9. Retrieved from http://www.thinkinnovation.org/file/research/23/en/Toppeta_Report_005_2010.pdf

Tregua, M., D'Auria, A., & Bifulco, F. (2015). Comparing research streams on smart city and sustainable city. *China USA Business Review*, *14*(4), 203–215.

United Nations. (2014). *World urbanization prospects: The 2014 revision, highlights*. New York, NY: United Nations Department of Economics and Social Affairs.

Vanolo, A. (2013). Smartmentality: The smart city as disciplinary strategy. *Urban Studies*, *51*(5), 883–898.

Vlahov, D., & Galea, S. (2002). Urbanization, urbanicity, and health. *Journal of Urban Health*, *79*(1), S1–S12.

Weisi, F., & Ping, P. (2014). A discussion on smart city management based on meta-synthesis method. *Management Science and Engineering*, *8*(1), 68–72.

World Commission on Environment and Development (WCED). (1987). *Our common future* (Vol. 383). Oxford: Oxford University Press.

Woyke, E. (2009). Asia's smart metropolis. *Forbes*, *184*(5), 61–63.

Yongmin, Z. (2010). Interpretation of smart planet and smart city. *China Informatio Times*, *10*, 38–41.

Zhiping, W. (2008). The application of wireless city technology in public administration. *Journal of Chinese Poeple's Armed Police Force*, *24*(1), 24–25.

# 4

# SMART CITY THEORIES AND MODELS


## ABSTRACT

*The theories and models of smart city make up the systemic approach that governs its readiness. This contains the in depth analysis of the concepts of the smart city as it relates to the environment as wells as the energy present. Several theories are modelled into the smart city system to guide its implementation and consideration among the construction professionals in the constitution industry. Subsequently, frameworks are not neglected in terms of their relationship between the outcome of the theories and models propounded and conceptual integration in human, technology and institution. Inferences are made from these theories and models, and thus decision-making are dependent on the visibility envisaged.*



**Keywords:** City framework; city models; smart city application; smart system; urbanisation; smart concept


## CONCEPT OF SMART CITY

Smart City is an innovative ideology in the management of a city. Its services and infrastructural characteristics and attribute have not been definitely defined adequately by anyone, although there are varieties of definitive terms used by many to describe what its concept could be. However, two significant variables have been identified to comprehensively explain the main components smart city must put into. The first variable is emphasised on the urban internet of things while the other on the interconnection of all aspects urban components. Most urbanised areas are faced with problems ranging from infrastructures, social and institutional peril. From the definitions of different authors, infrastructures are core to smart city concept and systematic technology application to them results to what is a smart city relates to. In other word, technology drives and enables the smartness behind any smart city. It is therefore the combination of these variables that is fundamental to Smart City. Smart City concept, therefore, is a comprehensive approach to the management and development of a city. It involves balancing technology, economic and social factors variables in an urban environment. In other word, it is a holistic approach to solving urban problems using new technologies to redefine the relationships among the stakeholders and urban models.

## SMART CITY THEORIES AND MODELS

Different theories and model have developed theories based on systems science generating hypotheses about the role information technology (IT) plays in the application of these theories to the development of cities. Diverse concepts and techniques towards becoming a smart city are numerously available for adoption. Wikipedia reveals that smart cities generate over 30% of greenhouse gases worldwide. These cities are challenged to provide solutions to the problems. The measures to be taken to make any city smart should not serve a sole purpose of environmental appearance but focus on economic, internal social, spatial distribution, designs and structure. A smart city is recommended to adopt IT to improve the service efficiency and social life of the people. New technologies should be explored because of their benefits directed especially towards the interest of the general public and the conservation of creative freedom in public spaces. Generally, in order to implement smart ideas, there is utmost need for the active participation of the general public. Skills are required to handle with care new technological tools, especially regarding data management and data security. Above all, synergies should be developed across all the systems within the city to enhance the achievement of the objectives smart cities by using resources with caution and hence provide an environment worth living in for the present and future generations.

Smart cities ideologies are gradually and intelligently solving some major challenges faced globally in terms of climate change and scarcity of resources. These challenges include global warming, transportation and education systems, etc. These and other challenges are targeted with the concept of smart city with the goal at aiming towards sustainability and general functionality. This is stated in relation to improving general quality of life among urban dwellers, and also bring changes inclined in territorial populated environment as it influences continues to be on the rise. Smart cities do not just come out of thin air, there are some intelligences that are associated with its concept. Several forms of intelligence behind the principles of smart cities can be demonstrated in some ways described below:

1. *Orchestration intelligence*: This is the intelligence integrated with another as establishments of institutions and community-based facilities towards solving challenges faced. Here, there is a combination of concepts and principles being fused together to function complementarily as functional unit towards identified challenges. Example of such collaboration is the Bletchley Park where the Nazi enigma cypher was decoded by a team led by Alan Turing.
2. *Empowerment intelligence*: In communities where infrastructural facilities are not within the expected standard in order to be identified as smart cities or communities, there is a provision of open platforms system coupled with establishment of experimental facilities in order to bring into reality smart cities among such communities. This intelligence is further described as developmental intelligence as it empowers (develops) a particular district to that standardised. Examples of this intelligence can be found in Cyber Port Zone in Hong Kong, and Kista Science city in Stockholm, Sweden.
3. *Instrumentation intelligence*: A smart city that experienced this intelligence is a product of data collection carried out in real time. This data is then analysed and predictive modelling is subsequently deployed across city districts. Inferences from which intelligence is obtained from the outcome of data analysed. However, this is subjected to the amount of data collected and the effectiveness of the analysis carried out. As expected, there is controversy about the effectiveness of this intelligence especially with regard to how surveillances work in smart cities. Example of this intelligence is its implementation in Amsterdam, the Netherlands.

In becoming a smart city, the first step to be taken is at the strategic level or area. This level encompasses every concept, principle, understanding to be deployed in actualisation of the city to be executed. After the level mentioned, other areas are also considered as they are listed below and represented in Fig. 4.1:

1. Administration.
2. Economy.
3. Energy and environment.
4. Environment.
5. Politics.
6. Quality of life.

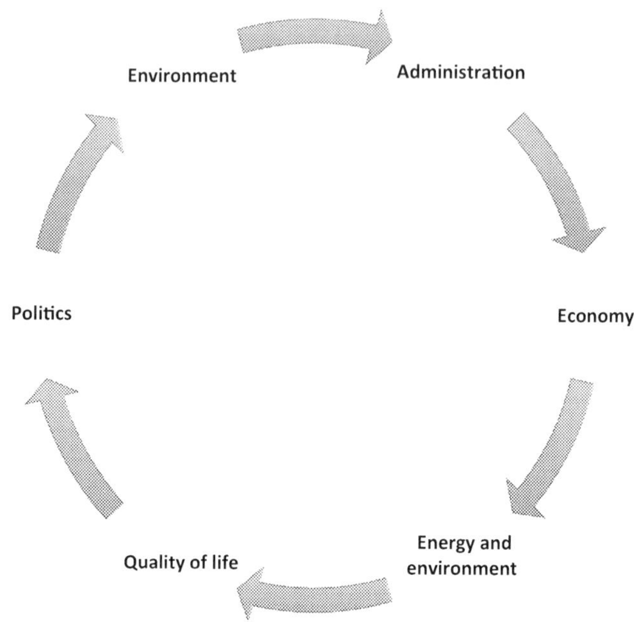


**Fig. 4.1. Some of the Levels of Becoming Smart City.**

In working towards a smart city, several factors are considered before it can be actualised. Some of these mentioned above are expressed in line with total conformity to designed plans and whole life cycle expectant from such city. Achieving a smart city can be viewed under the following variables discussed below.

## ENERGY AND THE ENVIRONMENT

Every city looks forward to and concerned about smart energy consumption by reducing energy usage, smart raw material consumption through efficient resource management, intelligent networks and monitoring systems, highly well-designed supply and disposal systems, etc., these are very important processes that drive change, technological developmental advancement, functional infrastructures, energy channels and efficiently sustained environment. These are achievable though; take for instance, smart grids for smart energy consumption and introduction of intelligent networks and monitoring systems to monitor the amount of energy generated per designed unit, the ones stored and that consumed within a particular time frame calculated. Smart meters record actual energy consumption for transparency and monitoring. These and many more function towards being informed about the amount of energy used within and outside the environment.

## MOBILITY

Smart mobility is attainable by introducing innovative traffic control and transport system that conserve resources and preserve the natural environment. The introduction of these systems will help in maintaining orderliness as we aim to preserve the environment to its closest advanced state. There are also modern digitalisation for maximum efficiency, affordability, productivity in terms of accessibility of the transport systems in order to achieve a settlement urbanised, compact within designs.

## ECONOMY

Smart economies by actively supporting formal education, research work and entrepreneurial skills, innovations, productivity and flexibility, and continuous knowledge acquisition and transfer, as well as local and global networks should be incorporated into the existing economy system. Smart economy drivers such as IT enterprises, energy and environmental service agencies should be encouraged.

## GOVERNANCE

Smart governance should be adopted to promote people's governance, planning and coordination processes, and encouraging public participation in decision-making processes. Smart governance can start from not only making smart fiscal policies but also those that could sustain the present and the future all at once and long run.

## SOCIETY

Quality of life should be greatly improved upon through provision of qualitative education, adult education, improved health, safety of individuals, preservation of culture, plurality of society and social cohesion. Creative instincts of people should not be neglected and sound thinking should be promoted. The opportunity to be presented daily in a smart city environment should encourage dwellers want to be smart as individuals and not just being an onlooker in the smart environment. The urban lifestyle should be platform for inspiration which foster competence to getting better than what was perceived. Well-designed considerations ticking all the boxes in human development will not only be about a smart city but also smart people dedicated towards improvement and creativity. Smart city is built on the concept of sustainability, and it is flexible in that it recognises resistance and move beyond it in conceptualising functionality directed in a path designed. To accurately describe and explain the concepts associated with Smart City, it is vital to bring into understanding its specifics through some specific frameworks. These frameworks are divided into three main dimensions which are expressed in technology, human and institutional frameworks.

## TECHNOLOGY FRAMEWORK

Almost all the concepts of the Smart city rely greatly on the use of technology; the technology to be used has to be in line with whatever aspect of smartness it is meant to cater for. When a city is smart technologically, it is a combination of different technological infrastructures, such as, information, virtual, digital cities, intelligent city and ubiquitous city (U-city) working together as a system. This is beyond a concept and it is solely for the purpose of connecting the community through up-to-date communication infrastructures, such as cyberspace, flexible service-oriented computing infrastructures making it easy to use any available devices to connect to them and creating innovativeness and standard services that can meet the needs of everyone; citizens' employees, governments and businesses. Technology framework is further classes into digital, virtual, information, intelligent and U-cities. They are expressed below.

### Digital City

When describing digital cities, they are the ones that fuse together infrastructures, technologies and digitalised tools into making cities within a set design. These kinds of cities thrive well on the influence of technological innovations and deliveries to bring enhancement in the quality of life of the residents, values in respect to the whole life cycle with regard to the designers, and sustainability in terms of economic impact. According to Yovanof and Hazapis (2009), it is defined in the aspects of having infrastructures that satisfies the government and relevant employees, masses and platform for business improvement through flexible innovative services combined together. Digital cities can connect many residents or citizens together through interconnection of information available to everyone at once or in subsequent time. Relationship is a great gain in building towards digitalised cities aimed at improving standards in every aspect of development.

## Virtual City

A virtual city is that its interface is nothing physical but in the cyberspace. It provides the channel for interaction between city dwellers and certain reality where operations are interconnected. It brings into practice the concept of hybrid city and real components where citizens come together for the purpose of living in a virtual environment devoid of physical entitlements. However, the virtual environment created is not the one devoid of people but of physical technology accessories in cables, connections and so on. The idea here is to eliminate physical proximity in order to maximise human potential as much as possible without interference with the physical.

## Information City

This is collecting local data and information to be available for public consumption. This city serves as a centre point for collection, distribution and management of information in the public. In this city type, many of the people living there are able to use the internet because of the information made possible through the medium of digitalised tools and technologies which in turn propel development as information passed are distributed across different sectors of developmental programmes. This city works in bridging the gaps among many connected embodiments in solidifying relationships, interactions and provide a linkage especially in areas where population is tensed. The functionality of the socio-economical and relevant economics is enhanced as there is a better interconnection among populace in civil services, the government and its officials as well as the entire population present within such city.

## Intelligent City

An intelligent city is not only smart; it also brings smartness in every sphere. This city can conveniently serve as one where there is dissemination of thoughts, analysis of planning and its consequential inferences coupled with technological research opportunities that aids further development. Here, creativity is always welcomed and there is always a transfer of knowledge in whatever forms it comes. Not only is human capital very important in this type of city, modern technologies are taking over operations as humans seek to solve its insatiable nature. Without no doubt, this type of city is filled with infrastructures that blends perfectly with technologies implemented with an option of upgrade to latest ones in order to fulfil more the desire to bring sustainability and transfer of knowledge as it outgrows its initial competence. In implementing intelligent city, many factors have to come in place synchronically for effectiveness. These factors ensue in the capacity of the design and the intended populace, the skills and availability of technologies with upgrades and relevance in time, government fiscal and long-term policies among others. However, in a situation where there is a platform for gradual input of the factors mentioned into the city system, it will function in terms of increase in performance as it beats radical innovations to working towards improving daily life which is in contrary to Komninos (2013) where emphasis was on its innovation as a radical concept rather than benefitted increase in functionality.

### Ubiquitous City

The concept of this city is to make available connections in every facet of the targeted environment. *Availability* is the golden word in this type of city. U-city serves as an extension to an already established digital city where there are accessibilities to facilities, infrastructures, information (data), technological advancements with the aim of adding more value. And like every other cities, there is ease in connection and availability of any devices with that of the citizens and its immediate environment. This city is set to be *perfect (or near perfect)* as it is structured to offer services in any forms across any surfaces. The services expected from this type of city qualifies it to function as a total package of digital, virtual, information, intelligent cities with regard to actualising concepts embedded into the concepts of the cities above. While the other cities might visualise, U-city brings into reality visualisation of mirages into what is desirable now and what is extended beyond present creation.

## HUMAN FRAMEWORK

Human infrastructure has to do with creative jobs or professions and voluntary organisations workforce, knowledge networks, etc., and this is vital for city development. Its variance includes, innovative city, learning city, humane city and knowledge city. This framework involves providing social infrastructures like culture and arts, education and training, business and commerce, etc., in order to build skilled workforce to enhance competitiveness in the global knowledge economy and eventually exploiting these human potentials to promote knowledge economy and innovation processes.

## Creative City

In creating a smart city of any form, creativity is always at its peak throughout every phase of implementation. In order to create a smart city, the designers must exhibit creativeness so as to obliterate obstacles that might stand against its success. A creative city is an epitome of the creativeness of the designers into what the citizens can relate to. A city that is creative brings connection between the parties (producer and consumer) involved from the conceptualisation of the smart city idea to where it is executed. There are always infrastructures that represent the social construct of the city envisaged as each city is an excerpt of the culture fused into modernisation. Apart from culture infused into its considerations, there are others to be considered that spread across education, psychology and business that are peculiar to the residents of the environment. Creative city is supposed to be loaded with avenues and platforms that will allow for creative ideas. Not only is this aimed at functioning towards a city, but also it should be centred in the area of modernisation where creative is the order of the day.

## Learning City

In a study carried out by Moser (2016), a learning city is expressed as it works in improving skilled workforce. This city learns all it can from creative city and targets the skilled workforce present as this will make development faster. The unskilled workforce is not totally neglected even as it covers minute aspect of the learning city concepts. From what is learnt, there is bound to be competition in general knowledge acquired, products and services offered, and effectiveness in other aspects of realisation. A learning city connects ideas and people together in smartness as it furthers to lead from existing practices as it strives to propound theories that could enhance interaction in every aspect of interaction and development.

## Humane City

A city without humans is desolate in every facet, and that involves humans without efforts put in place to bring establishments and upgrade is as good as having nothing present in it. Therefore, the humans' workforce is essential in executing set out designs and plans for better quality of life. The workforce in this city could focus on educating as many as possible with the target being pointed towards getting a city vast in knowledge of disciplines spread across different functions. The attention is focussed on increasing the level of higher educated people which in turns builds intellectually enhanced individuals within the system. This is agreed to bring further development in every aspect of the city's communications and development as it works in the line of smartness and sustainable infrastructures. Humane city is also the one where sanity is expressed without much hassle. This implies that concepts and practices can be projected and analysed with the highest form of reasoning. The result of this event brings attraction into such city. Just like a city developed and equipped with various modern facilities, companies, firms, organisations and sorts will migrate in order to add more values to it while lesser developing areas are deserted. This stressed the need to make development 'go round' across most cities as smart cities shouldn't be restricted (limited) to some regions while others are left to ruin. As some cities are becoming Smart; it is expected that Smart people are going to dwell there. Rather than concentrating this smartness into some cities, migrations should be done to the lower cities so as to develop them to bring more Smart cities which in the long run help in total development.

### Knowledge City

In a publication by Deakin and Allwinkle (2007) where they discussed the regeneration of urban cities and sustainable communities, the knowledge amassed during the course of executing a concept function helps immensely as it brings the roles of networks, innovation and creativity in building successful partnership in an identified community. Even when there is very much similarities between this city and that of learning and educating cities, there is a difference however in their outputs. While learning and educating cities amass knowledge, knowledge city brings such knowledge into innovations for execution. It is safe to say that learning city precedes knowledge city. The higher the knowledgeable the humans are in such city, the better the direction towards enjoying benefits that comes with residing in Smart cities.

## INSTITUTIONAL FRAMEWORK

Caragliu, Del Bo, and Nijkamp (2009) defined that a city is smart when there is enormous investments in infrastructure social, human, capital and IT. These are the factors that enhance quality of life and fuel sustainable growth through a governance style that employs citizenry participation. Moser (2016) opines that Smart city is a strategic means to broaden the use of IT and members of the cities with the help of relevant authorities (different institutions and governments) with the targeted goal of enhancing and improving the use of IT in order to improve daily quality of life. Institutions across various techniques develop principles that could work in Smart cities and specific roles attached. The initiatives of Smart cities are like *salt bridge* in technological advancements in improving social, economic and general ramifications as we tend towards better and faster services in time. The better the relationship between the people of the community and the government, coupled with other institutions, the better it goes in improving such community and everybody in it. Institutions can work hand in hand with the people to develop construct and find solutions to challenges facing the community, such as traffic congestion, flood, social amenities, air pollution and so on.

## CONCLUSION

Digital city, virtual city, information city, intelligent city, U-city, creative city, learning city, humane city, knowledge city and other cities require functional theories and models in order for the systems in them to work. This can be aided by the implementation of government and private policies that can aid in speeding the growth of cities. In achieving urbanisation, priorities should be given to this aspect of the smart city execution so as to be able to create designed and targeted values.

## REFERENCES

Caragliu, A. Del Bo, C., & Nijkamp, P. (2009). Smart cities in Europe. Serie Research Memoranda 0048. VU University Amsterdam. *Faculty of Economics, Business Administration and Econometrics*, 4(2), 124–146.

Deakin, M., & Allwinkle, S. (2007). Urban regeneration and sustainable communities: The role of networks, innovation and creativity in building successful partnerships. *Journal of Urban Technology*, *14*(1), 77–91. doi:10.1080/10630730701260118

Komninos, N. (2013). What makes cities intelligent? In M. Deakin (Ed.), *Smart cities: Governing, modelling and analyzing the transition* (p. 77). London: Taylor and Francis.

Moser, M. A. (2016). What is smart about the smart communities movement? *University of Calgary Journal*, 1, 10–11. Retrieved from www.ucalgary.ca

Yovanof, G. S., & Hazapis, G. N. (2009). An architectural framework and enabling wireless technologies for digital cities & intelligent urban environments. *Wireless Personal Communications*, *49*(3), 445–463. doi:10.1007/s11277-009-9693-4

# PART 3

# SMART CITIES STAKEHOLDERS

# 5

# SMART CITIES TEAM MEMBERS


## ABSTRACT

*In defining smart city and its effects on the citizens, the ideas and generalisation of the team members that makes up the smart city team must be thoroughly considered. It is one thing to have the concepts and processes on ground on smart city, it is another to have qualified team members that can deliver such city within a targeted standard. Stakeholders, construction professionals, citizens, concerned individuals among all make up the smart city team members. These members can also be spread across disciplines in order to facilitate effectiveness in every activity designed. Activities such as dissecting characteristics, control and management of smart city are controlled by these team members as they seek for maximisation of output from the resources available.*



**Keywords:** City team members; developmental efficiency; Smart city management; Smart city stakeholders; Smart policy; Urban city


## INTRODUCTION TO SMART CITIES TEAM MEMBERS

The term 'smart city' has been viewed by the generality of researchers, stakeholder companies and the informed public as the integration of government policies, information technology (IT), communication sensors, environmental responsiveness, lower emission and more efficient use of natural renewable resources to improve existing infrastructure and also the quality of life of all citizens in that city. According to Harrison et al. (2010), many of the global cities of previous ages have been overtaken by the recent trends of globalisation;

therefore, for a city to remain globally relevant, it needs to improve the quality of life of her citizens, and one of the ways through which it can achieve this is by improving its services and management of its resources.

## DEFINITIONS OF SMART CITY

In some studies, Bakici, Almirall, and Wareham (2012) and Barrionuevo, Berrone, and Ricart (2012) see smart city as involving extensive use of technology to develop sustainable habitation and increase quality of life. While Marsal-Llacuna, Colomer-Llinas, and Melendez-Frigola (2014) focussed on their definitions on the social–economic impact of using data, IT and new thinking paradigms integrated into human life to provide greater efficiency in service delivery to citizens of the smart city.

Nam and Pardo (2011) made the following six propositions on the concept of smart city as related to governmental agencies and policy-makers:

1. That smart cities should not only be viewed technologically but also socio-economically. Indeed, Rohracher (2001) states that a socio-technical view to the study broadens the technological policy and integrates innovation with sustainability and sociability. This means that it is not the same effort that goes into developing a new automated tool or piece of utility that should be put into smart cities given that human lives and living are involved.
2. That smart cities rather than being driven by systems are to be service-oriented. Therefore, if a system will enhance better integration but offer poorer service delivery, it should be less prioritised for one which will provide better service delivery.
3. When thinking of smart cities, they should not be thought of in terms of big or large urban cities alone but in effect the whole nation or state or even the world since the goals of smart cities, such as better quality of life, lower gas emissions and access to better health care to mention but a few are the goals of the United Nations.
4. Smart cities have to do with multisectorial partnership and integration and it is not mono-sectorial in nature meaning it does not just have to do with IT alone, but employs a whole lot of disciplines including architectural, remote sensing, traffic management, etc.
5. Whereas in the case of a technological change, we may have a revolution in which certain ways of doing things are almost immediately taken away

and new ways or items flood the market, smart cities change do not work with such instant change, rather they evolve. The phrase 'Rome was not built in a day' applies to smart cities because those who live in smart cities must be smart citizens to enjoy the benefits it offers. Hence, long-term strategies which will keep being developed and implemented are some of the ways to making a city smart.

6. Smart cities should be considered as a harmonisation between the material world with its physical attributes of location, structures, distance, direction and time and the virtual or immaterial world. The use of intelligent systems will definitely cause some of the above attributes to be less impactful than they have been all our lives, yet they will be the basis on which these intelligent systems will operate.

## CHARACTERISTICS OF SMART CITIES

Giffinger et al. (2007) highlighted the following factors that make up a smart city. These characteristics are also used to asses a given city's performance as a smart city:

1. *Smart Economy*: This refers to how competitive the economy is and includes the following factors:
   i. *Innovative Spirit*: This has to do with the driving force for innovation in the economy and can be measured through the following indicators:
      a. What percentage of the gross domestic product (GDP) of the city goes into research and development?
      b. What is the employment rate in sectors that require intensive knowledge?
      c. How many people apply for patient rights among the inhabitants of the city?
   ii. *Entrepreneurship*: This can be measured through the following indicators:
      a. What is the self-employment rate?
      b. How many new businesses are registered per year?
   iii. Economic image and trade mark can be measured through asking how important the headquarters is as a decision-making centre.

iv. Productivity is measured through the GDP of every employee in the city.

v. *Flexibility of Labour Market*: This is measured by determining the unemployment rate and the proportion of the population that have partial or part-time employment.

vi. *International Presence*: This can be measured by asking:

a. Are companies with their headquarters in the city quoted on the national stock exchange?

b. What is the volume of the air transport of workers into the city?

c. What is the volume of the air transport of freight into the city?

2. *Smart People*: What is the level of human capital and it includes the following factors:

i. *Level of Qualification*: It is the city known as a top-level knowledge centre either through its research centres or universities. Questions arise on what the population of the city is and also that it must have a minimum international standard classification of education (5–6) years which relates that the citizen should be a graduate of a tertiary institution or have advanced research qualifications. Another question is to know the level of foreign language skills possessed by the city's populace.

ii. *Affinity to Learning and Life*: What is the participation in lifelong learning per resident over the total population of the city? How many books do each resident loan per year? What is the level of participation in learning language courses?

iii. *Structural and Ethnic Plurality*: What percentage of the city are foreigners? and What percentage of the city are nationals who are born abroad?

iv. *Flexibility*: What is the perception of the populace towards getting a new job?

v. *Creativity*: What is the percentage of the population of the city who work in industries or manufacturing companies that are involved in creative ideas and products?

vi. *Open-mindedness*: What is the attitude of the people towards elections? What is their turn-out like? Does the populace accept foreign nationals? Are they immigration friendly? How knowledgeable are they about the people of the world around their nation?

vii. *Participation in Public Life*: What is the level of participation in elections, city hall meetings?

3. *Smart Governance*: Peoples' participation in decision-making in matters that affect the city:

   i. *Participation in Decision-making*: How many city representatives does the city have? What is the level of political activity of their inhabitants? What is the level of gender balance in the city representatives? How important is the political clime of the city to her inhabitants?

   ii. *Public and Social Services*: What is the percentage of children in day care? What is the population of the city in old people's homes? What is the quality of the schools, hospitals, prisons and available in the city?

   iii. *Transparent Governance*: Are the populace satisfied with the fight against corruption? What is the level of transparency of bureaucratic functions in the city?

4. *Smart Mobility*: How easy can information be accessed and transport accessibility?

   i. *Local Accessibility*: What is the network of public transport per citizen of the city? How satisfied are the inhabitants with their access to public transport and with the quality of public transport?

   ii. *International Accessibility*: How accessibly is the city to other nations? Does it have an airport, a seaport or water way?

   iii. *Availability of information and communication technology (ICT) Infrastructure*: what is the share of the populace that have computers in their houses? What percentage of the inhabitants have broadband internet in their homes?

   iv. *Sustainable, Innovative and Safe Transport Systems*: Includes use of electric cars, economical vehicles, traffic safety, encouragement of the use of bicycles and walking.

5. *Smart Environment*: Protection of the natural environment and smart usage of natural resources:

   i. *Attractiveness of Natural Conditions*: How many hours of sunshine does the city have and how is it being utilised?

   ii. *Environmental Protection*: What is the general value of the inhabitants on environmental protection? What are the steps taken on an individual level to protect the environment, such as gardening, tree planting, etc.?

iii. *Sustainable Resource Management*: This involves efficient use of water and electricity calculated per GDP.

6. *Smart Living*: Has to do with the quality of life of the population:

   i. *Cultural Facilities*: Visits to cultural sites and recreation centres can be calculated to determine the quality of life of the city inhabitants.

   ii. *Health Conditions*: Check the life expectancy of the population, ratio of health workers to the population, the availability of ultramodern health facilities and the satisfaction of the inhabitants with the quality of the healthcare system in use.

   iii. *Safety Conditions*: Check the crime rate, the level of kidnapping and armed robbery are the people satisfied with the level of security provided by the city?

   iv. *Housing Quality*: Percentage of houses that are sustainable in their construction, how satisfied are the owners with their personal houses, what is the average living area per inhabitant, how balanced is the living space?

   v. *Education Facilities*: How satisfied are the inhabitants with the quality of the city's educational system and facilities? How accessible are the city's educational facilities? How many students enrol in the educational institutions? What is the student or teacher ratio?

   vi. *Social Cohesion*: What is the level of poverty among the city inhabitants?

   vii. *Tourist Activity*: How important is tourism to the populace of the city?

## MANAGEMENT OF SMART CITIES

Management is the act of handling or controlling something successfully. It can also be defined as the skilful handling of resources for reuse for the purpose of creating value.

Nam and Pardo (2011) stated that failure to manage high risks lead to total collapse in any public sector project that is technology driven. Management forms the non-technical side of any innovative smart city and the effectiveness or efficiency of management of technological infrastructure will lead to the success or failure of such a smart city.

## STAKEHOLDERS INVOLVED IN THE MANAGEMENT OF SMART CITIES

Newcombe (2003) identified two areas of interaction between project stakeholders and the project:

1. *Cultural Arena*: Identified stakeholders such as project team who share the vision and values of the vendors and such shared values could be used as a basis to propose changes. They seek the common good of the project yet may subject it to some changes.
2. *Political Arena*: Consists of individuals and interest groups which are deemed to be powerful, and exert high influence on the success of the project.

The researcher further stated that each group has expectations which pressure on the vendors of the smart city to fulfil. Not being mindful of this turned a decade long railway project in Germany to be heavily spoken against due to mounting expenses when commissioned.

Laartz and Lulf (2014) believe that improved communication is a key ingredient in the evolving of smart cities; they opine that technology vendors of smart cities and the local government leaders can encourage the development of smart cities. In a study that they carried out, they discovered there is a gap in shared understanding between smart city technology vendors and local city officials on the requirements for smart city development. Going forward, they propose that more time given to pursing a shared understanding from the local business environment, citizens, local city officials and technological vendors before creating a smart city solution.

Petri and Guarise (2015) undertook a workshop to explain the general objectives and the specific goals of the smart city initiative which was divided into specific objectives and work-groups. Making the people part of the innovation of their city and helping them to own the vision of the smart city development and increasing their awareness on the development with exhibitions of some of the advanced technologies that will be operated by the city.

In the Netherlands, for example, strategic stakeholder's engagement is employed in development of smart cities in which different relevant stakeholders break off into various working groups to include fields, such as software developers, accreditation agencies and energy performance consultants (Cullen, 2014)

Laartz and Lulf (2014) identified the following areas of improvement necessary for the acceptance and adequate management of smart cities on the part of the vendors:

1. Focus of vendors' presentations should be shifted from what their product can do to how to integrate it with the existing systems.
2. Having more than one proprietary solution. In cases where there is a collapse of the operating system of any of these technological cities, it will also mean the collapse of the city, if not the death of its citizens. As a result, a variety of technological solutions from different firms seems to be better than just one solution from one firm.
3. Better integration will prevent innovation in one part of the city life which will bring a stalemate to innovation in another part as may be determined in the future.

While on the part of the city officials and users:

1. Understanding on the part of the city officials of the importance of so many departments working together to help provide data for the smart city technology providers. For example, a traffic project in a city required 13 different government agencies input.
2. Development of smart citizens, who will understand the concept of smart cities, know the requirements, and the do's and dont's of smart cities.

Barrionuevo et al. (2012) pointed out key areas to focus and analyse when drawing up a strategic plan for the management of smart cities:

1. *Economic*: A smart city's economy can be determined by deciding frameworks to locally develop businesses and SMEs in major areas of economic development being forecasted, such as ICT, biotechnology, etc.
2. *Human Resources*: For sustainable smart city development, investment in human resources through the existing institutions of learning and creation of new ones with more specific focus cannot be overlooked.
3. *Environment*: A deliberate environmental policy with follow-up actions that lead to a cleaner, pollution free, natural resource preservation and renewable energy utilisation to be put in place. Examples of cities working with such policies already are Malaga in Spain and Moncton in Canada.
4. *Social Cohesion*: Through community development, improved health care, emergency management and public governance.
5. *Urban Planning*: a lot of campaign is going on for allowing the natural environment to be preserved; this includes allowing more green areas

instead of car parks and pavements, use of smart lightening and renewable solar panels as street lights, tree planting, banning tree cutting, green road medians, etc. Cities are now being named according to their functions, such as industrial parks, IT hub, etc.

6. *Governance and Civic Participation*: Everybody should be involved in the process. There should be proper awareness and passing of information about smart city concept between the government and its citizens.
7. *Public Management*: With the wave of private public partnership and other private funding initiatives, more room is being given to the private sector to participate in the management of public utilities which can be done faster and better.
8. *Transportation and Mobility*: Geographic Information Systems (GIS) and remote sensing are improving the way in which transportation and mobility are being taken. Cars are enabled with maps and tracking devices to enable them recover from getting lost, on the other hand intelligent bus systems and train systems are being employed by large cities in China, with high speed on the go maintenance at the stations.

## TECHNOLOGICAL MANAGEMENT OF SMART CITIES

ICT when integrated into a city's service delivery system transforms it into an intelligent manager of the cities resources. By incorporating ICT into city development, interconnecting physical infrastructure with social infrastructure, and business infrastructure is known as virtual city infrastructure. Virtual city infrastructure is a network of sensors, processors, transmitters, and accompanying software which gather, integrate, analyse and optimise data to improve the quality of decision-making and increase the general intelligence of the city (Harrison et al., 2010). Cities that run on technological applications bring out more opportunities for research work attracting new innovations and a commitment to development. Bakici et al. (2012) opined that in managing smart cities, using Barcelona as an example, one ought to develop a network management platform which will incorporate communication sensors and other types of sensor data. Some researchers at IBM see technological management under three divisions (Harrison et al., 2010):

1. *Instrumentation*: The following equipment are used to collect live data in real time; video surveillance cameras, water quality sensors, loop detectors, radio frequency identification detectors for payment of tolls smart electric and water metres, telematics for roads and trains, water

quality sensors, water level monitors for sewers, GPS on mobile phones, GPS systems on vehicles, etc. Indeed internet-enabled mobile phones can act as means of instrumentation through social networks like Facebook, or YouTube, can send live events to an information pool for onward action especially in an emergency, such as kidnapping, armed robbery or accident. Instrumentation is most advantageous for financial transactions such as billing; other uses are in monitoring, optimisation and adjustments.

2. *Interconnection*: For a city to be smart, there are needs for interconnectivity among its various sectors and agencies. There should be a logical connection between many of the IT software used by different agencies within the city to help manage and operate the city services and also improve the quality of life of her populace. Harrison et al. (2010) posits that information from instrumented systems is brought into a service-oriented architecture environment which contains multiple resources and has a job of interconnecting that information with the point of execution for various city services.
3. *Intelligence*: This involves the integration of various information into models which according to Harrison et al. (2010) is: flexible, extensible and can process multistep analytical simulations; automatically adjusts itself to the required function, visual or has visual output as it has strong effect on the user, standardised with recognised global standards.

Barrionuevo et al. (2012) cited Brazil, Rio de Janeiro, a city resolved to engage the use of ICT in managing disaster and flood after floods hit that city in the fourth month of the year 2010. Such technology can control city traffic flow, public transit systems and power outages with emails, short message service, alerts to the public on impending disaster and how to handle it but will need to have high speed internet broadband services using fibre optic cables.

## MANAGEMENT OF GOVERNMENT POLICIES OF SMART CITIES AND EDUCATION OF SMART CITIZENS

Bakici et al. (2012) stated in his work that smart cities will include programmes that will train people in digital literacy. Chourabi et al. (2012) stated that such education allow citizens of the city to participate in the governance, and management of the city since they are also active users or end users of the process of evolution of a city into smart city status. The reason for the education of the citizens is that smart cities fare better through participatory governance and individual responsibility.

Barrionuevo et al. (2012) opines that private firms are ideal for leading the way in the development and construction of smart cities. To this, other public institutions and universities can collaborate.

## CONCLUSION

There is a need to take a holistic approach to the provision of smart cities solutions all around the world. Also, using an intelligent index to monitor smart cities initiative as stated by Marsal-Llacuna et al. (2014) can further bridge the gap between vendors of smart cities and the end users. Giffinger et al. (2007) together with Harrison et al. (2010) gave us a benchmark of indicators to improving smart cities; a critical appraisal of each city in the light of these benchmark indicators can greatly enhance the management of smart cities. These indicators have to be governed by experts; and they are expressed in the competence of smart city team members handling such city.

## REFERENCES

Bakici, T., Almirall, E., & Wareham, J. (2012). A Smart City Initiative: The case of Barcelona. *Journal of Knowledge Economics*, *4*, 135–148.

Barrionuevo, J. M., Berrone, P., & Ricart, J. E. (2012). Smart cities. Sustainable progress. *IESE Insight*, *14*, 50–57. doi:10.15581/002.ART-2152

Chourabi, H., Taewoo, N., Walker, S., Gil-Gracia, J., Mellouli, S., Nahon, K., … Scholl, H. Understanding smart cities, an integrative framework. *Proceedings of HICSS, 45th Hawaii, conference.*

Cullen, A. (2014). Building energy rating schemes. Accessing issues and impacts. A report by the Building Energy Efficiency Taskgroup (BEET) of International Partnership for Energy Efficient Cooperation.

Giffinger, R., Fertner, C., Kramar, H., Kalasek, R., Pichler-Milanovic, N., & Meijers, E. (2007). Smart cities – Ranking of European medium-sized cities. Final report. Centre of Regional Science, Vienna, UT. Retrieved from www.smart-cities.eu. Accessed on October 20, 2017.

Harrison, C., Eckman, B., Hamilton, R., Hartswick, P., Kalagnanam, J., Paraszczak, J., & Williams, P. (2010). Foundations for Smarter cities. *IBM Journal of Research and Development*, *54*(4), 1–16.

Laartz, J., & Lulf, S. (2014). Partnering to build smart cities: Better communications between local government leaders and technology vendors can encourage the development of connected, resource-efficient urban area. *Global Institute of Open Data/IT*, *44*(1), 44–60.

Marsal-Llacuna, M., Colomer-Llinas, J., & Melendez-Frigola, J. (2014). Lessons in urban monitoring taken from sustainable and livable cities to better address the Smart Cities Initiative. *Technological Forecasting and Social Change*, *90*, 611–622.

Nam, T., & Pardo, T. A. (2011). Conceptualizing smart city with dimensions of technology, people, and institutions. In *Proceedings of the 12th annual international digital government research conference: Digital Government Innovation in Challenging Times*, College Park, MD (pp. 282–291). doi:10.1145/2037556.2037602

Newcombe, R. (2003). From client to project stakeholders: A stakeholders mapping approach. *Construction Management and Construction*, *21*(8), 841–848. doi:10.1080/0144619032000072137

Petri, A., & Guarise, A. (2015). General objectives and the specific goals of the Smart City Initiative. Retrieved from https://smartcities.ieee.org/news-bulletin/january-2015/the-ieee-smart-cities-initiative-in-trento-italy.html. Accessed on October 12, 2017.

Rohracher, H. (2001). Managing the technological transition to sustainable construction of buildings: A socio-technical perspective. *Technological Analysis and Strategic Management*, *13*(1), 137–150.

# 6

# SMART CITY TEAM PARTNERSHIP


## ABSTRACT

*When there is a cordial relationship among the members of the smart city team, there are bounds to be achievements and executions of projects within stipulated time of the budget allocated. The partnership in ideas and overall discipline will propel the activities involved in executing smart cities in the world. In identifying not just the definitions of smart city, the developmental aspect of the concept is considered across phases of construction as the industry strives towards elegance and advancement. However, exciting as it comes in benefits and enhancement in the quality of life, several problems have also been identified albeit opportunities are somewhat presented in the challenges when analysed thoroughly from the inception to completion. The interaction within team members across countries will pave way for collaborators into the system.*



**Keywords:** City team partners; Smart city development; Smart city stakeholders; Smart infrastructure; Smart policy and economy; sustainable development


## INTRODUCTION

Construction recently has turned a new face; the development in the industry bought about the innovation of the buildings and environment so as to avoid rapid urbanisation or ways of settlement. Taking into consideration the social, economy and environment of settlement, cities has been seen as a system or way of life that can aid the success of becoming smart. Smart cities are means used in developing the economy and development of environment, this city is used to monitor and produce alternatives use of important infrastructures, such as land, buildings, information communication technology (ICT), factories, etc. Since population have been increasing over time the need to expand cities and their development brought about the innovation of smart city, making life easy and affordable with the use of available resources.

Recently, in the late twentieth century, the term smart city is centred to increase easy and interesting environment in terms of technology and communication by different industries for the proper use of urban spaces. In addition to this, old existing structures cannot stand the text of time and some new structures are not constructed to suit the taste of people and their environment. Nevertheless, they cannot be pulled down or destroyed the creation or invention of smart city draws a link between the new ideas or innovation and existing infrastructure and tends to improve social, economy and environment. The cities are also claimed to protect the interest of economic competitiveness and increase standard of living for urban population endlessly. The force of the smart cities is the involvement of governance and public participation, having to make intelligent decisions and create strategy level of becoming smart. This process includes careful decision on long-term partnering implementations and not only the individual project but also the involvement of the people in the community.

In conclusion, Smart city is all about community and the people; the community must be conducive for people in terms of transportation, traffic control centre, road and urban planning. It looks into the global challenges, that is, wastage, scarcity and change in the use of resources. However, smart cities help to improve the standard of living, brought about progress in the use of technologies and efficient use of available resources.

## DEFINITION OF SMART CITIES

According to Giffinger and Gudrun (2010), smart city is a city built to perform different functions which have various characteristics. It comprises of different endowments, ideas, free access, innovations and improved standard of living in the environment. Moreover, smart cities are seen as unique tools or techniques or ideas of connecting physical infrastructure, social infrastructure, business infrastructures, technology innovation and ideas together in order to make a great environment for the users as buttressed by Hartley (2005).

Toppeta (2010) also defined smart city as a city designed and planned to improve technicality, create new ideas, developed innovation and provide solution on complexity cities so as to improve the standard of living and enhance sustainable environment through the combined services of ICT, Web 2.0 technology and other design organisations. Moreover, this idea gives a stable infrastructural component and service of a city, such as real estate, mass housing, health care, access road, networking, education, administration, public services or utilities, security and well organised environment as cited in Washburn et al. (2010).

In conclusion, smart city is where the production, distribution and uses of energy, information and communication, mobility and transport or road network are intimately linked together to develop the city.

## SMART CITIES DEVELOPMENT

Smart cities is an invention connecting people, financing and availability of mass housing, energy generating and distribution, improve quality on service work, social amenities and infrastructures, technologies involvement, accessing easy transportation, use of local and available materials to achieve a sustainable construction and development and promote good quality of life and improve standard of living.

However, three keys are the betterment of urban planning and management, growth of the economy and advancement on ICTs in order to meet the needs of the society. The three keys are as follow:

### Economy

Government is a very important element in nation building, anything that needs establishment has to pass through the approval of the government and following the policies and laws of the nation. Smart governance encourages modification in government, coordination and planning processes with private and public participation. Implementation of construction projects contributes a large percentage to the economy development of the country. When there is a quality production in construction designed by the administration, it will bring an understanding that will help in developing collaborations within different economy sectors, private and public organisation units and thereby promote business and production of goods and services in the communities. Also, there are enhancements in quality research work and their usage through the help of ICTs and use of widely available public digital data to enable the involvement of people, end-users and members of the communities to partake in the public decision-making process, participation of local authorities and involvement of people within the community or urban areas.

Finally, the growth of the economy is characterised by the involvement of people, private and public sectors or organisation and government.

### Environment

A healthy living or quality of life is dependent on the environment. The air, water, land, climate change, topography, natural resources, etc., are all important in developing a smart city. The environment we live has a great influence on our day-to-day activities as human beings. A conducive environment will enhance productivity and encourage a flexible way of life. Smart cities are actively in support of a better environment for people and their communities by creating more institutions for learning and carrying out research work, construction and connection of land, air and water movement, promoting business, generating and distributing energy, development in the use of ICTs, mass housing, convenient environment, waste management, use of available natural resources, etc.

### Society

Culture, beliefs, norms, rules and regulations, policy, health, government, social issues are important aspects in developing a smart city. The innovation of smart city is basically more of the technicality it brings, but also socialisation since the participation of every individual or person in the environment is essential and the needs of the society is taking into account. In achieving a smart life or city, the civil societies, local government authorities, the elders, leaders and rulers must come together and focus on the safety of the people, their cultures and ethnic values, health, education, mobility and easy access within and outside the environment, relaxation centres, business growth and training and social unity.

## PROBLEMS OF SMART CITIES

Population over time cannot be overemphasised as this result to increase in settlement across the globe. The difficulty faced in settling down and getting a sustainable environment brought about the idea of smart cities. It was basically introduced to provide solutions to loss of functionalities: poor management scheme, inadequate resources, pollution, poor healthcare facilities, congestion, poor road network, obsolete infrastructures or buildings or utilities as sourced from Toppeta (2010) and Washburn et al. (2010). Clean water, energy, sewage or refuge disposal, consumption of goods and services and free licensed land are limited or scarce at our disposal. The largely increased number of populations already occupies the urban spaces, making settlement difficult for people which leads to poor networking between humans and there day-to-day activities since individuals has to decide their own way of living. Climatic change over time has also been a major issue that is yet to be addressed as the reign of global warming, extended heat waves and floods. Smart city also take into considering the issue of globalisation in terms of road network, information, institutions and information technologies.

Moreover, the belief of the stakeholders differ from one another which leads to different problems as different stakeholder are involved with different personal interest, social and political influence, divers motives, level of understanding, benefit involvements as effect on the development and new innovation of Smart Cities instead of improving the technical, physical and sustainability of the environment as sourced from Taewoo and Theresa (2011). However, changes made on the economic, social and environment structures should be welcomed and adopted. The changes are positioned between struggles and cooperation.

## OPPORTUNITIES IN SMART CITIES PROJECTS

1. Availability of water supply.
2. Availability and affordable accommodation.
3. Accessible road network, public transport and mobility.
4. Information technologies.
5. Sustainable environment.
6. Institution.
7. Safety and health.
8. Good governance.
9. Communication and digitalisation.
10. Security.

## FEATURES OF SMART CITIES

The innovation or idea of smart city is to solve the problem of urbanisation or settlement. The development of smart city occurs when infrastructure and vision have been realised or accomplished. Some of the characteristics are as follows:

1. It enhances physical dimension.
2. Majorly developed on larger environmental areas.
3. It is service oriented.
4. The development of smart city is a concept of socioeconomic development.
5. Smart city is the combination of multisectorial one.
6. It is a natural or global movement.
7. It is evolution not revolution.
8. It brings harmony between material and virtual worlds.
9. It accommodates rapid urbanisation.

## TEAM MEMBERS, PEOPLE AND PARTICIPANT INVOLVED IN THE CREATION OF SMART CITIES IN SOME COUNTRIES

The partners involved in the creation of smart cities vary from one country to another. This chapter will specialises on countries who are members of the United Nations (UN) around the globe. It is believed that individual member or organisation can contribute to the strategy development of the city, but the barriers lies in the structure of the council not being able to deploy the strategic approach to be carried out which often time face delays in project delivery since the involvement of different partners are involved in the project. However, if a project team can assist the council in organisation or managing and rationalisation on the project at appropriate time, cost and quality delivery will be quick and effective within stipulated budget and plan.

According to the United Smart Cities Project in 2014, the partners involved in the innovation include participants from both public and private partnerships. However, some of these partners are listed as follows in identified countries:

## United States of America

According to the publication made by the Roll & Carriero (2013), smart cities projects and associated members are categorised into three different dimensions that gives a template that can be used by the countries under the UN. The three forms of partnership and members involved in the creation of smart cities are seen below:

1. Principal project partners.
2. Associated project partners, that is, institution or education sector and private sector organisations.
3. Cities and citizens involvement.

The principal project partners are as follows:

1. *The United Nations Economic Commission (UNECE)*: The organisation is aimed at promoting economy, environment and society for a sustainable development among the 56 within Europe and United States. However, countries participating or members of UNECE and involved in the creations of Smart Cities and partners of the new innovation.
2. *The Organisation for International Economic Relation*: This organisation serves as an intermediary and adviser between the public and private sectors; they are more interested in the public interest and offers offerings and requirement to the private sectors. They are also involved in promoting multistakeholders network globally to maintain projects and development relating to economy, environment and society, urban development programmes and smart cities, education, agriculture and health.
3. *The UN Habitat*: Since population is rapidly increasing all over the world, the general assembly of the UN in late 1970s begin to handle the issues of urban growth, cities and people settlements and creation of awareness on urban development processes. The UN Habitat is a programme aimed at building a better urban future in order to promote social, economic and environmental suitable settlements and availability of adequate shelter.
4. *The International Society of City and Regional Planners (ISOCARP)*: The institute of ISOCARP is an association of experienced professional planners throughout the globe. The association was established in the year 1965 in order to bring recognition and experienced qualified professional planners together internationally in not less than 80 countries globally. The association is aimed at improving cities and territories through proper planning practices within the countries and their environments,

trainings, research from various fields and quality enlightened through the educational system.

5. *The Royal Institution of Chartered Surveyors*: This is an international institute where over more than 100,000 professional members and experienced elite in handling property, land and construction of both building and civil projects comes together to form a body. This body helps in maintaining professional standards and profound quality education to regulate and promote the profession, they are trained to protect the client's and consumer's interest through the code of ethic and laws governing the body, they also give impartial advice, make analysis and achieve value for money through proper guidance.
6. *The Environmental Agency Austria*: This is an expertise body on environmental issues and the largest in Austria. This is a private partner working to create a better and conducive environment by constructing bridges between the economy, political and social at both national and international levels. The agency has over 450 experts who are trained in 55 academic disciplines making them the best in providing an environmental solution worldwide.

The Associated Project Partners, that is, institution or education sector and private sector organisations are as follows:

1. *Academia*: Institute of Technology, Zurich, Switzerland.
2. *Private Sectors*: Reach-U, Estonia, OIER (bringing private sector members together to support and partner both in the implementation activities and financial planning of smart cities), Energy Sectors and International Council for Local Environment Initiative.

*Cities and Citizens Involvement*: The acknowledgement of the end-user will make the innovation a success, which is why the other stakeholders involved should be within the communities. The stakeholders include:

1. Private sector and relevant industry.
2. National government.
3. City planners, managers architect, engineers and quantity surveyors.
4. Academia and research institute.
5. Local authorities and city councils within the participating cities.
6. NGOs and SGOs.

## India

In a brochure given by the Indian smart cities development, the collaboration between central, state and urban local bodies are the participating stakeholders. The project groups discuss the viability of the projects, innovations and technologies and considering different ideas that can be used to enhance the project and save costs. Cross-sector groups can also be established, through meetings and presentations, and these can submit and execute holistic innovative solutions to broader urban issues. Such a synergistic approach will also make it possible for the city to connect and accelerate progress. It can also look at ways to strengthen previous activities, thus making existing projects smart.

However, the funding of the creation of smart city in India can be through: own sources, grants, viability gap funding (by central government) and private public partnership.

The potential partners or collaborator for Smart Cities in India are:

1. Government agencies or ministries.
2. Industry association or federation of industry bodies.
3. Private companies.

The people or team involved in India Smart Cities:

1. Architect.
2. Urban developer.
3. Safety and health.
4. Government bodies.
5. Policy integration.

## Australia

According to Michael (2014), in the publication made by the Australian Smart Communities Association (ASCA) strategic plans, the association brought three together to major frontiers in order to participate and embrace new innovations:

1. The first the group was the 40 local councils in the country.
2. The second are the members of the Australian smart city association and lastly 25 leading companies involves in infrastructure, utilities, telecoms,

sustainability, research and development institutions, health, education and information communication technologies.

3. The third is the collaboration or partnership was to provide leadership to lead the development of the modern cities to be suitable, organised, share responsibility and transparent economy.

In Australia, the collaboration with local council has helped the country and members of smart city association to know what the community and people or end-user's needs the most and so as to deliver smart city project that will benefit the people economically, environmentally and socially. The collaboration with top leading companies (industries, stakeholders like transport, education, health and communities) will encourage the council to implementation their own local smart cities development.

Finally, the environment and people are what makes a city smart, it is basically the need or expectation of people; the association (ASCA) visits people or city to know their need thereby capitalising on it to make the city smart.

## United Kingdom

According to the publication made by Centre for Cities (2014), in the UK, about 8% out of 100% of the population lives in the cities. Smart city is an important part of the world; the UN in 2008 recorded that half of the world's population settles in the cities and predicted that the settlement will improve to 70% in the year 2050. The UK government is working on how the cities can become smarter and sustainable for citizen although challenges like restructuring, unemployment, increase in urban populations leading to pressure on transport and housing, climate change, pressure on public finances, awareness and creation of the new innovation, etc., are facing the idea of smart cities in the country. Nevertheless, the government in the UK are involved in helping cities in response to the challenges by assisting in the development of smarter cities because of the economic, social and environment benefits for the government and end-users since smart city is worldwide and opens opportunities for business. In 2012, Business, Innovation and skills department with the support of the government commissioned smart cities standard strategy for smart city solutions. In addition, the department helps to give guidelines in making decision; developing smart cities for the public, private and professionals involved in order to transform cities to smart cities and the ability to meet the end-user expectation. Also, they also came up with smart city framework (SCF) which helps in developing new innovations and strategies continuously. The SCF was also structured in a way that the future of UK cities is more effective, sustainable and efficient in the nearest future. However, the leadership and governance, business model, culture and improvement of stakeholders in the creation, delivery and use of the smart cities in terms of services and convenience can be added benefits when there are implementations from structured concepts agreed upon by the SCF stakeholders. The people of the community have to be carried along whenever a structured design is to be implemented. This is to facilitate even distribution of information and compliance with laid down rules and regulations.

It was stated in the publication and indicated the roles and involvement of people:

1. *The Community*: They are the most important in the construction of the smart cities due to the fact that they are end-users and the city is to be developed based on what they want in the community in terms of social, economy and the environment development. Being the prime audience, the involvement of the following members cannot be over emphasised:

   i. Policy developer authority renders their services in terms of design, commissioning and delivery role.

   ii. Local authorities (Elected Leaders, Chief Executive, Directors and Officers of key department.

2. *The Stakeholders*: The involvement of other stakeholders interested in the leading and developing the city environment. The following are the stakeholders involved in executing the project:

   i. *Promoter*: The senior executives in private firms or organisations who are ready to partner with the body or government.

   ii. *Consumers*: Community representatives and residents who work and live within or visit the city.

   iii. *Deliverers*: Leaders in tertiary institution or education sectors, business and suppliers.

   iv. *Investors*: Leaders of voluntary sector organisations, those that are active within the city such as financial institutions.

   v. *External*: People who are affected directly or indirectly, such as central government, local government and public sector organisations.

3. *The Government*: The participation of government and leaders helps to ensure a clear accountability within the city authority, have control over

city leaders to make sure there is an effective governance arrangements from the inception to the completions level, gives a broad based leadership team to oversee the project across the city, organising a formal programme management disciplines and encourages a transparent and open governance to the public.

## Europe (London and Dublin)

Europe is one of the larger continents in the world. The idea of smart cities in the nation has been rooted in Dublin and London since it is has a massive population. Since early 2000s, the countries have been participating and improved by reducing congestion on road thereby encouraging people to use motor cycle as a means of improving their health by keeping them healthy, generating energy and creating street lighting, increasing use of technology (predicting weather condition) and production of smart phones, smart buildings (improving building performance), accommodating environment, etc., nevertheless, there are limitations in delivering smart cities which then leads to the involvement of stakeholders from powerful public and private sectors who will see to the hard and smart infrastructures, economy, social, environment and political system in the city and regional.

However, it is important to develop how to achieve the new innovation after the challenges, which include, fear of change, culture, cities engagement, cost and budget, whereas the diversify participation of the stakeholders involvement is another major issue. In Europe, it was suggested that there should be collaboration between the internal and external stakeholders.

1. *Internal Stakeholder*: The government, local authorities, public sectors and the people behind the ideas of smart cities, that is, researchers.
2. *External Stakeholder*: Examples of external stakeholders are the relevant companies, universities, citizens, civil societies, policy-makers and institutions.

There is need for long-term partnership between the stakeholders from different sectors so that the objectives and values of smart city will be established. In order to achieve this aim of collaboration, there are three important models of governance that governs the participating stakeholders:

1. Systematic network governance between different participating stakeholders.
2. Hierarchic governance based on power, influence and control.
3. Market governance on prices, transactions and efficiency.

Jamie (2016) establishes the fact that it is best to introduce governance model for group of stakeholders which will guide them in the right situation and right action. The collaboration model was developed because of the difficulties in keeping up with new technology innovations and resources management and usage, and this leads to the developing of top tech companies and incredible research centres thereby setting up 40 key advisory network leaders to direct the establishment. The network leaders help to achieve the vision and strategy for smart Dublin and they meet twice within a year to check if the development is in right direction, look forward to more opportunities and create rooms for togetherness between them as leaders.

## CONCLUSION

The idea of smart cities is for everybody to innovate together; it is no sort of separate entities but group of organisation, people and communities as part of the ecosystem. It should be practiced by everybody in order to enhance country growth. There is need for understandable roles of citizens, government and stakeholders should be established, continuous connection between the interdependent stakeholders. The social, economy, environment, citizen's engagement, civil society and energy smartness should be encouraged or enhanced in both rural and urban region for easy growth within the speculated time. It is not only government's push but also highly of stakeholders and investors.

## REFERENCES

Centre for Cities. (2014). Cities Outlook. Retreived from https://www.centreforcities.org

Giffinger, R., & Gudrun, H. (2010). Smart cities ranking: An effective instrument for the positioning of cities? *ACE: Architecture, City and Environment*, *4*(12), 7–25.

Hartley, J. (2005). Innovation in governance and public services: Past and present. *Public Money & Management*, *25*(1), 27–34.

Jamie, J. D. (2016). Gauging America's Retirement Income Planning Literacy: A Method for Determining Retirement Knowledgeable Clients. *Journal of Personal Finance*, *15*(1), 7–8.

Michael, W. (2014). Australian Smart Communities Association (ASCA). Retrieved from www.australiansmartcommunities.org.au

Roll, G., & Carriero, D. (2015). Global Smart Cities Project: Smart urban solutions for countries with transition economies and developing countries. Project Documnet. United Nations Economic Commission for Europe (UNECE). Retrieved from https://www.unece.org/fileadmin/DAM/hlm/projects/SMART_CITIES/United_Smart_Cities_Project_Document.pdf.

Taewoo, N., & Theresa, A. P. (2011). *Smart city as urban innovation: Focusing on management, policy and context.* ICEGOV2011, September 26–28. Center for Technology in Government University at Albany, State University of New York, New York, NY.

Toppeta, D. (2010). The Smart City Vision: How innovation and ICT can build smart, "livable", sustainable cities: The Innovation Knowledge Foundation. Retrieved from http://www.thinkinnovation.org/file/research/23/en/Toppeta_Report_005_2010.pdf

Washburn, D., Sindhu, U., Balaouras, S., Dines, R. A., Hayes, N. M., & Nelson, L. E. (2010). *Helping CIOs understand "Smart City" Initiatives: Defining the smart city, its drivers, and the role of the CIO.* Cambridge, MA: Forrester Research, Incorporation.

# PART 4

# SUSTAINABLE DEVELOPMENT (SD)

# 7

# SUSTAINABLE DEVELOPMENT: DEFINITION AND PRINCIPLES

## ABSTRACT

*The major goal when transforming a city to smart city is to achieve sustainability. Sustainable development (SD) has been talked over the years with several industries considering the principles attached. Also, for a functional smart city planning, considerations must be anchored on sustainability that can be achieved through digitalisation and advancement of technological tools. The contradictory discourse of sustainability in SD, contemporary challenges of the concept of SD, drivers of SD, innovation and SD, thinking about innovation and technology, how companies manage innovation, barriers to smart cities development and others highlight what to be discussed in this chapter.*

**Keywords:** Digitalisation; Smart city definition; Smart principles; sustainability; sustainable development; urbanised city

## INTRODUCTION

In defining sustainable development (SD), several ideas have been inculcated into what it really means in different aspect it is defined. In a definition that is proposed by Bruntland Commission, (Cerin, 2006; Stoddart, 2011) noted the commission's definition has been frequently used even now. Despite sustainability cutting across several disciplines, the functionality related to the concept has never been limited with full concentration on the scope it is targeted

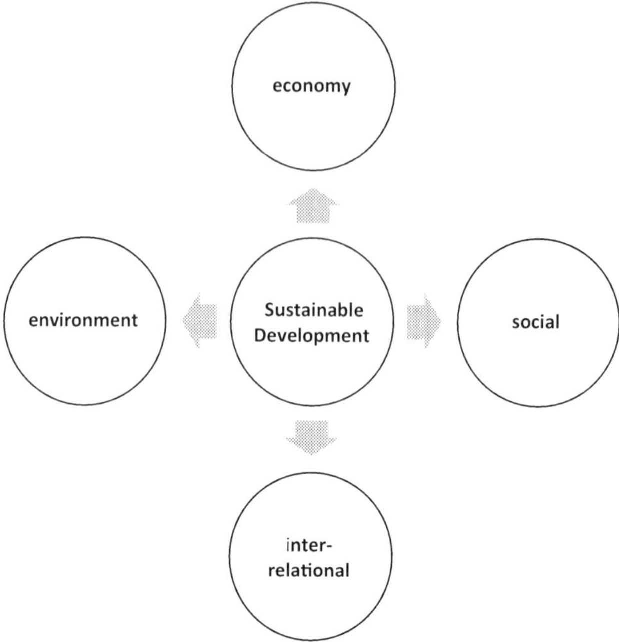


**Fig. 7.1. SD Survival Policies.**

towards. This diversified functionalities however explains the importance of the concept when inculcated into any discipline. The concept adopted into the construction industry aimed at satisfying the immediate environmental needs, as well as making provisions for the future with all considerations made today. SD offers survival of policies envisaged now coupled with expectations in economy, environment, social and interrelational adaptability towards decision-making as shown in Fig. 7.1.

The principle of SD can be challenged by a very important factor in capital. Capital is categorised into several types in natural, social and man-made. These arms of capital affect the level at which SD can be categorised. Despite working towards better project delivery so as to satisfy the demands of the clients, these factors (combined or in twos) create a channel that can determine the pace at which SD influences the structure it is meant to infiltrate. In classifying aggregate level of capital matters; weak SD encompasses the infusion of manufactured or man-made capital to natural capital. This type of categorisation procures that man-made or manufactured capital can be an alternative to the natural one. On the other hand, the strong SD recognises the dominance of the natural capital with little or no consideration to the man-made or manufactured capital in terms of being an alternative or substitute.

Identifying the better of the two categories has been hectic over the year with different opinions on which is perceived important. A study by Stoddart (2011) pointed that ecologists and environmentalists in large number favours the strong sustainability definition and its corresponding principles.

## THE TERM: SUSTAINABLE DEVELOPMENT

SD is a term used across several disciplines. The word 'sustainability' has been trending for some years now as professionals see it fit to discuss implementing it into every activity put into production, processing and maintenance. It is arguably coined from SD but with much emphasis on identified structures related to the construction industry. In the construction industry, recent efforts have been directed towards making it a normal standard for every part of construction process. As early as when reconnaissance is carried out, through the implementation of value management practices and workshops to delivering projects within budget sum and duration, sustainability has been attempted to improve whole life cycle of structures, getting the best value, and putting considerations for the generations yet unborn. As versatile as it is, the mode of operation differs according to various ways it is been set up. This is simply illustrated in the construction industry that works in line of value, cost, satisfaction and reuse.

## THE CONTRADICTORY DISCOURSE OF SUSTAINABILITY IN SD

In defining exactly what sustainability is in respect to what SD entails, arriving at a precise position on the subject is as difficult as putting the relationships between the two words into concise understanding at the same time. In simple term, it is quite challenging putting to certainty the origin of sustainability from SD without having contradictory opinions from professionals in several industries mainly concerned with the term.

The Table 7.1 gives a summary of the views of some professionals with regard to what sustainability entails across various sectors of human economy.

## DEVELOPMENT AND SUSTAINABILITY

It is evident the presence of sustainability in SD. The meaning has been expressed over the years and the ways it is perceived differs across disciplines

Table 7.1. **Different Perceptions on Sustainability.**

| S/N | Author | Sustainability |
|---|---|---|
| 1 | Acselrad (1999) | In biological sciences where capital or stock is the main attraction in establishing flow of biomass without comprising capital for the people directly attached to it |
| 2 | Bossel (1998) | Sustainability is observed in making considerations about the threats and opportunities in the future that addresses dimensions in:<br>1. Political<br>2. Material<br>3. Psychological<br>4. Ecological<br>5. Cultural<br>6. Environmental<br>7. Legal<br>8. Economic<br>9. Social |
| 3. | Waguespack and Surovell (2017) | Maintaining conditions or providing greater ones in an ecosystem for the present people while considering the ones after them |
| 4. | Barbosa, Drach, and Corbella (2014) | Pointed that sustainability seeks balance between human's needs and that of the environment. It is further identified as the relationship between friends and foes of different values and needs. Also, sustainability dynamism in process of change that encompasses concepts subdivided into five dimensions: social, economic, ecological, geographical and cultural |

and value expected to be achieved. In line with this, the concept of sustainability explains the way at which sustainability is coined from SD and the simplicity it brings in terms of understanding and knowledge drafted from its numerous benefits towards the construction industry and any other industries at large. In relation to the fundamentals of SD in elements, development and sustainability are experienced before any relative concept can be put in place. These elements must follow each other consequently to achieve stability of the goals in view. In a study by Sharpley (2000), development and sustainability can be placed side by side as they follow each other in sequence. There is no contradiction whatsoever and benefits from the two elements can be channelled to function not just as separate units but also singularly as the construction industry tends towards having constructions that are sustainable. Development and sustainability are like twins that cannot be separated. This implies that for one to occur, the other must be present (there is absence of development without sustainability and sustainability would not kick off without development) (Sachs, 2010).

In classic economics developmental theories, development is seen as growth in the economic development of a particular phase from traditional aspect to contemporary ones. The transformation could be swift or takes time depending on how fast developmental theories are implemented within a specific time frame. Table 7.2 gives the summary and comprehensive list of some of the perceptions of various theories related to the subject.

## CONTEMPORARY CHALLENGES OF THE CONCEPT OF SD

From the inception of development and sustainability, there have been different definitions and theories that try to explain the terminologies. These disparities

**Table 7.2. Different Author's Theories on Development and Sustainability.**

| S/N | Author | View on Model |
|---|---|---|
| 1. | Todaro and Smith (2003) | Identifies developing countries in terms of their limitation in allocating available resources due to the following reasons:<br>1. Rigid government policies<br>2. Prevalent corruption among government officials<br>3. Inadequacy in executing economic activities due to inefficiency and limitedness<br>4. Instabilities in political, economic and institutional policies<br>5. Dependence on foreign countries and policies |
| 2. | Willis (2005) and Remenyi (2004) | Improving the quality of life and self-sufficiencies in economic practices through contemporary knowledge that are dependent on global feasibilities and integrations |
| 3. | Tangi (2005) | Creation of liveable environment for the residents where the quality of life is at its peak |
| 4. | Romer (1986) and Todaro and Smith (2003) | Economic growth is an output of internal state or corporate system channelled coupled with the essentiality of knowledge and ideas. Their theory is further expatiated into four parts:<br>1. Capital measured in units of consumer goods<br>2. Individual skills in terms of labour<br>3. Human capital comprising education, learning, development and individual training<br>4. Technological development |
| 5. | Thomas (2004) | Experiences felt in the past, relived now in all positive forms by a society in every form of history and growth |
| 6. | Jenkins (2009) | Maintaining consistency in a process over a period of time within available resources |

create an avenue for contradictions in terms of perception, criticisms and general overview of what SD entails. In the construction industry, the adoption of the practice has been slow. Most of the construction industries prefer the concepts that answers the demands expected now with few actually working towards sustainability. This is most expedient in developing countries where emphasis is on what is now within a set budget and policy, and the developed countries working towards what is next within a set budget, policy and satisfaction. The challenge expressed in adoption and other challenges are stated below:

1. SD involves participation of the government, non-governmental firms, stakeholders and other subsidiaries without prior understanding of the execution of the practice to locals which constitutes the majority.
2. The competitiveness and development rate between developed and developing countries widens as adoption of SD put the former at a greater advantage.
3. SD focusses more on technological development with neglect to basic human problems in poverty, pestilence and so on.
4. The development associated with sustainability is determined by the government policy-makers and sometimes decisions made are not favourable.
5. The adoption if sustainable developed has improved the environment in terms of value but it has not stopped deterioration of the environment in the total sense (United Nations Environmental Programme, 2012).
6. Difficulty in implementing SD practices into major industries despite the availability of standards, protocols, policies set to govern its implementation.

## DRIVERS OF SD

### Innovation and SD

Technology has come to stay. The benefits that come along with implementation and full adoption into firms and construction industry (or any industry at large) bring excitement in many ways. These benefits are directed in bringing better quality of life and satisfaction to humans and possibly positive changes in the environment. Not only has technology help in sustaining available resources across several factors, it has gone to improve the quality and quantity of goods and services rendered per unit time while human efforts are minimised. Andrew (2000) gave an insight of the changing experienced today as an output of discoveries in telecommunication and transfer of information through mediums made possible in technology. In this process, solutions are manufactured swifter within the shortest timeframe.

Despite the excitement that comes with technological advancements in project execution, delivery and management, it is obvious that the influence of technology as digitalised tools in innovation and sustainability is huge, it is however visible that it also comes along with challenges that has to be solved in order to counter contradictory opinions with regard to implementation and adoption especially in the construction industry. In order to curb these challenges that resulted from different factors across several phases in the project planning and execution, construction firms have centred their attention in working towards approaches that correlates with SD in the areas of ensuring understanding among participants of the construction industry, enhancing project performances by introducing modern concepts, and setting goals that are worked upon realisation. The concept of sustainability inculcated into project will help in addressing difficulties in bringing smart designs and technologies into the industry, promoting faster growth in general development, and risk management policies. With all these and more in place, the client is most times convinced of the competence and functionality of the construction professionals in identifying possible errors from the previous projects and providing solutions to them without repetition.

## Thinking About Innovation and Technology

Smaller firms tend to operate in an operation that can make them bigger in sizes, structures, productions, satisfaction and so on while the already big ones will fancy the opportunity of getting better in all ramifications. In doing so, wider audiences (clients) have to be reached and values created within a set scope of work and contract. The ever increasing effects of internet in economic activities generally are evident in connection and transfer of information from one continent to the other. While trying to reach the untapped audience (client), provisions have to be made in order to cater for the client's demands particular to a location. Satisfying these demands call for thinking beyond a known concept which is technologically inclined. Not only are construction activities will be improved, the relationship and market value of the participants involved in the project are enhanced tremendously too.

### How Companies Manage Innovation

In observing the commitment of firms towards implementing SD into activities, the innovations by which the concept of SD established can be observed along with approaches to challenges and barriers in recognising and creating opportunities. In a study carried out by Andrew (2000) where managers of firms were approached, 88% of them agreed that in driving a firm to moving forward, SD is an important key, while 83 of those approached asserted that in achieving mission and vision statement of a firm, SD ion of such firms can never be underrated. Furthermore, the staffs of these firms were required to take into account SD where 55% of firms inculcated SD into environmental and social matters and 28% into environmental matters only. The delegation of functions expected in SD within these firms shows the firm's commitment in managing SD expectancy and the closeness of these firms towards integrating process that put SD within set innovation process.

## BARRIERS TO SMART CITIES DEVELOPMENT

In building smart cities, several factors have to function together with little or no challenges. However, there are times where development will be delayed by barriers foreseen or unprepared. Smart cities are back bone to a country's economy and such must be catered for to outsmart every form of redundancy that might present itself now or later. The smart cities target improvement in quality of life of the residents, and sustainability in terms of the environment. It can never be neglected that the complexities that come with smart cities will bring some complications in implementation. Since most population is driven towards urbanisation, there is a need to provide conceptual practices that will clear the path for the possibility of smart city in order to achieve development envisaged.

In identifying barriers that could be faced in smart city development, it is right to understand how they will affect activities by which it is going to be employed. Some of the barriers are listed below:

1. Difficulty in executing complexity of smart city system.
2. Disparity in the economic policies.
3. Difficulty in the innovation of technologies.
4. Limited social interaction about the smart city system.
5. Differences in opinions on what the concept entails.

6. Restrictions by the government.
7. Legal and regulations.
8. Cost of implementation.
9. Information and awareness.
10. Sustaining smart city concept in the long run.

## FURTHER BARRIERS TO SMART CITIES DEVELOPMENT

### Economic Sustainability

Economic sustainability is best understood as sustaining the economic environment in order to generate wealth. The total wealth to be generated depends on many factors. Two of the major factors are the capacity and size of the economy influenced. It is possible for an economy to be big without having the capacity to cater for all the necessities required from a standard economy. Such economy is bound to lack fast paced growth and stability. In order for the economy to be stable at all, capacity should be the number one factor to be considered when determining the concept that would work with a designed or already established economy. The economic environment encompasses the factors embedded within the economy that could directly or indirectly affect the gross domestic product (GDP) of a country or firm. These factors are centred in the population growth, availability of skilled man-power to carry out sustainable practices, location of the economy, level of education, attracting investment and mortgage services, capacities in taxing and other development payment made and controlled by several organisation bodies.

Smart city brings to understand the nature of the economy being operated. Also, the system at which the economy functions is better understood when smart city principles are instigated into planning and all. This will allow for proper designing of models that would work easily within and outside the set goal of the economy. But in a situation where the planning is opposite, it would be difficult and practically pointless in making models that would function seamlessly. For a city to have a boosted economy, there must be a cordial relationship between the public and the private companies, firms and so on. This relationship is expressed in the development of public private partnership where diversity is enjoyed in making and maintaining economy sustainability. In a process where there is no understanding of what the economy entails particularly the financial aspect of it, crisis is always the first and consistent challenge that will be experienced. The economy must be stable enough in order for it to be sustainable. This should never be skipped and considerations must be well analysed when propounding what and what will be put together in order to making inferences on whether to go fully into a smart city and its development.

## Social Sustainability

Social sustainability simply explains the interaction of the society with the situations experienced before and the ones presented now. There is always a fear of caste system whenever smart cities are mentioned among some populace. They are of the opinion that it is easy to create classes and groups which will separate the people of such particular society. The city officials must ensure stability in the distribution of wealth and information to everybody about what smart city development entails. In fact, models to be presented must be written such clarity that explains plans to be executed in improving social amenities especially driving towards improving the quality of lives of the entire population.

It should never be forgotten that the targeted beneficiaries of smart cities are the people in it. Concerned stakeholders must ensure implementation of designs without eradicating the culture of that society. Stakeholders must find a way of improving the city by inculcating what makes the society and what it is capitalising on making something great out of the uniqueness for everyone to enjoy. After all, a city united is a city that develops rapidly. All hands must be on deck to ensure that thoughts and plans are within what the society can relate and function to if any development is to be experienced rapidly.

## Environmental Sustainability

Social sustainability comes with putting the population first, environmental sustainability brings all attention to the interactions with the environment. It has been observed for years about environmental concerns currently facing development and the entire globe in various ways. There have been concerns about the increasing rate of these problems and how they affect humans and the environment. There is a limited availability of resources in water, food and quality in wholesome. Also, pressure arises on health of both humans and animals and this raises concerns among different stakeholders concerned with project delivery and smart cities developers. Other concerns are raised in flooding, hurricane, typhoon and so on as a resulted of the depleted ozone layer. The environment must be designed in a way that will minimise the rate of energy used and concentrate emphasis on efficiency across networks and amenities. This will be beneficial to both humans and the environment at the same time. Pollutions can be reduced when energy consumed is reduced and greenness is encouraged across various sectors of the environment. The technologies to be implemented into the environment must function to lower the damage already done and not aggravate concerns on ground. Value and risk managements can be integrated in building concepts and practices and the risks projected coupled with unforeseen circumstances can be catered for without much problem. Despite divided opinions whether digitalisation of cities into smart ones can deliver benefits mentioned and more, it is however never in doubt that implementation of technological concepts into building and infrastructural development will go a long way in improving cities as it drives into that which is not only habitable but sustainable at the same time.

## Same Objective but Different Challenges, Trends and Needs

Urbanisation comes with improvement on development from what it was to what is expected. Expectations come in different shades across several locations. The differences could come in the form of the government policies, topography of the location, water level, level of education, climatic conditions, heat exchange and so on. The pace of smart city development is dependent on the intensity of these factors and many more. Also, migration is experienced mostly from rural areas to urban areas. Therefore, the urban area is densely populated and so are the needs of the populace. In order to cater for this, different developmental concepts have to be put in place to meet the demands and needs of the people. While the urban areas are developing rapidly per unit population, the rural areas are developing at a pace from the scratch. Due to unavailability of existing structures on which SD can be built, it takes time, effort and cost in bridging the gap between the two areas.

## Economic Development and the Financial Change

Change is good. The changes that follow urbanisation in terms of city development is profound in ways that it can be positive and negative all at the same time. Take for example, Ogombo, a river side area of Lagos state, Nigeria has been experiencing massive development. The place has been continually filled with sand and modern infrastructures at erected. While there is a cheer in the development in terms of infrastructures, there is however a downside to it as many fishermen go out of stock. The dredged rivers once used to be fishing ground for the settlers of the area. The financial and economic situation of the place is affected immensely and the change experienced is either sweet or bitter. In considering urban productivity, the growth in efficiency of a city is determined by the availability of resources with the ability to get desirable outputs which creates income towards improved condition of living. This is similar to considering GDP of a city as a leading determinant of the productive urban areas. In situations where there is conflict of interest in GDP of the particular area, there is bound to occur challenges in accepting city development principles with regard to balancing effects on the economy and financial developments.

## CONCLUSION

Rapid rise in urbanisation coincide the rate at which SD is being discussed. In the construction industry, emphasis has been placed on having construction processes that follows the path of sustainable not just for the sake of today but also generations yet to come. The world is developing at a swift pace and materials are used daily to cater the ever rising demand of the people. In order to cope with this pressure especially in the built environment, smart city corroborates the ideal representation of SD and one of the most advanced at that.

## REFERENCES

Acselrad, H. (1999). Discourses of urban sustainability. *Revista Estudos Urbanos Regionals, Rio de Janeiro*, *25*(74), 79–80. https://doi.org/10.22296/23171529.1999n1p79

Andrew, D. (2000). Sustainable innovation: Drivers and barriers. *World Business Council for Sustainable Development*. Dearing/OECD TIP workshop, Chemin de Conches, Geneva.

Barbosa, G. S., Drach, P. R., & Corbella, O. D. (2014). A conceptual review of the terms sustainable development and sustainability. *International Journal of Social Sciences*, *3*(2), 1–15.

Bossel, H. (1998). Ecosystem and society: Orientation for sustainable development. Springer, Germany: Berlin. https://doi.org/10.1007/978-3-642-58769-6_25

Cerin, P. (2006). Bringing economic opportunity into line with environmental influence: A discussion on the Coase theorem and the Porter and van der Linde hypothesis. Ecological Economics, 56(2), 209–225.

Jenkins, W. (2009). *Berkshire encyclopedia of sustainability: The spirit of sustainability* (Vol. 1, 1st ed.). Berkshire: Berkshire Publishing Group.

Remenyi, J. (2004). What is development? In D. Kingsbury, J. Remenyi, J. McKay, & J. Hunt (Eds.), *Key issues in development Hampshire*. New York, NY: Palgrave Macmillan.

Romer, P. (1986). Increasing returns and long-run growth. *The Journal of Political Economy*, *94*(5), 1002–1037. Retrieved from http://www.jstor.org/stable/1833190. Accessed on September 15, 2015.

Sachs, W. (2010). Environment. In W. Sachs (Ed.), *The development dictionary: A guide to knowledge as power*. London: Zed Books.

Sharpley, R. (2000). Tourism and sustainable development: Exploring the theoretical divide. *Journal of Sustainable Tourism*, *8*(1), 1–19. doi:10.1080/09669580008667346

Stoddart, H. (2011). *A pocket guide to sustainable development governance*. Brussels: Stakeholder Forum.

Tangi, S. (2005). *Introduction to development studies*. Scientific Network Academia.edu.

Thomas, A. (2004). The study of development. Paper prepared for DSA annual conference, Church House, London.

Todaro, M. P., & Smith, S. C. (2003). *Economic development* (8th ed.). Harlow: Pearson Education Limited.

United Nations Environmental Programme (UNEP). (2012). Keeping track of our changing environment: From Rio to Rio+20 (1992–2012). Retrieved from http://www.unep.org/geo/pdfs/Keeping_Track.pdf. Accessed on November 4, 2015.

Waguespack, N. M., & Surovell, T. A. (2017). Clovis hunting strategies, or how to make out on plentiful resources. *American Antiquity*, *68*(2), 333–352. doi:https://doi.org/10.2307/3557083

Willis, K. (2005). *Theories and practices of development*. London: Routledge.

# PART 5

# SMART CITIES AND SUSTAINABLE DEVELOPMENT

# 8

# QUALITY OF LIFE


## ABSTRACT

*People will continue to migrate from rural to urban areas. This always results in congestion in the civilised part where there is contention for the resources available. Policies have to be made and implemented in order to counter scarcity and redundancy as most urban cities tend to halt in growth when population is beyond controllable size. Smart cities come into the frame by alleviating the present condition of the places to that which is convenient for everybody. Quality of life, meanings of smart cities, quality of life of smart cities citizens are the priorities when implementing smart city concepts into sustainable development.*



**Keywords:** digitalised city; life enhancement principles; smart city benefits; stand of living; sustainability; sustainable development


## INTRODUCTION

In recent decades, the rural–urban migration all over the world has massively increased beyond what can be easily checked. All over the world, the rate at which towns are turning to become cities by the reason of the population of indwellers has continued to raise points of concern. In a survey done by Thales (2012), it was recorded that more than half of the world's population currently resides in towns and cities. At the time of the survey, the world population was given to be 7 billion people, meaning that more than 3.5 billion people either live in town or in cities. In addition, a United Nations forecast has it that by the year 2050, the population of the world would reach 9 billion and the forecast added that more than 70% of the population will be living in the cities around the world (SDSN, 2013).

Such high indicators for more concentration of population in the cities as against the villages and towns, which boast of more land areas for comfortable living and cohabitation, has raised more concern in international discussion (SDSN, 2013). Among some of the concerns identified are issues of atmospheric pollution, overcrowding, traffic congestions, security challenges, increased crime rate, unemployment and lots more (UNRISD, 2013). However, one of the solutions posed to address this trend is improvement of citizens' quality of life, operating transport, security infrastructure in optimal fashion and building of competitive cities everywhere to secure a position among the world's top most attractive places to live (Shooshtarian & Ridley, 2016). All these were identified to be achieved using a comprehensive 'know-how' integrated system called a smart city.

A smart city is the city centred at encouraging sustainable development. It encompasses various definitions of concepts, principles, logics, interactions put together to enhance human technology relationship for an improved quality of life. Also, it entails bringing cities to be developed within digitalised tools and technologies fused into policies made by concerned stakeholders in the infrastructural industries. The consequences of this interaction between the components in the smart city aids in reducing waste, unnecessary congestion, pollution, redundancy among others. The city is made possible by fusing technologically advanced integrations in setting up qualities (schools, amenities, libraries, traffic system, etc.) and relating them with functions obtained through learned knowledge and networks.

Smart city is all about community and the people. It is concerned with the interaction that exists between the human component of a community and the entirety of the environment; the community must be conducive for people in terms of transportation, traffic control centre, road and urban planning. In a smart city, issues that relates to waste, allocation of resources, scarcity are well planned for and checked to ensure maximal optimisation and usage.

## MEANINGS OF SMART CITIES

Since the introduction and emergence of the phrase 'smart city' in the late twentieth century, various meanings have been attributed to its usage. From the name, it could be reasoned to mean a city that is smart in its doing, that is, a city that uses recent technologies in its operation and dealings, and which comprises people that move with the current waves of technological changes.

However, many definitions have been given in trying to explain what a smart city is and what it does.

Hartley, (2005) described a smart city as a unique technique or tool of connecting technological innovations and ideas together with physical, social and business infrastructures to achieve a more interesting environment for users. Hartley (2005) based the definition of smart city on the technology as it influences the decisions of people in employing the various environmental infrastructures to their advantages. Another definition is that of Giffinger and Gudrun (2010) which described a smart city as a city built to perform different functions which have various characteristics. Giffinger and Gudrun (2010) described it to comprise of different endowments, ideas, free access, innovations and improved standard of living in the environment.

In another definition, a smart city is associated to the interconnection of the dwellers and the incorporation of internet of things. Smart city is seen as a city management concept within which a city is holistically maintained and managed with ease. It involves balancing technology, economic and social factors' variables in an urban environment. In other words, it is a holistic approach to solving urban problems using the advantage new technologies to redefine the relationships among the stakeholders and urban model. Many words have been used in many articles and write-ups to describe the term, some of which are: wired city, intelligent city, hybrid city, creative city, informative city, learning city, humane city, etc. but the most widely used and acceptable are the smart and digital cities (Nam & Pardo, 2011).

## QUALITY OF LIFE OF SMART CITIES CITIZENS

The smart city technology has been traced to the days before the World War II. It was an invention tailored towards the Americans who believe in machines and equipment. It was then referred to as the Know-How City (Giffinger & Gudrun, 2010). After World War II however, many other developed nations have embraced this technology and has customised it to fit their local demand with the human populace as the centre of attraction and concern in the technological innovations. In driving home, the initiative, the construction industry has been saddled the major responsibility of creating an innovative and interactive human environment. Andamon (2005) opined that the functionality expected from the built environment is to satisfy the wants and needs of humans. In achieving better quality of life expectancy, concepts of smart cities revolve around sustainability, satisfaction and comfortability. The integration and interaction of these concepts would enforce rapid development in every ramification across practices designed to be relatable and controlled by the local authorities.

It is however necessary to hammer on the fact that in achieving a smart environment, the citizenry of such an environment has a lot to contribute (Andamon, 2005). Their contributions are majorly based on their perceived derivation from the system and this invariably increases their commitments to the technological environment. Some of the advantages derived from a smart city technology by the citizens' lifestyles as seen in the quality of life they live as discussed below.

## Time Loss Eradication

In smart technology, effective usage of time is of paramount importance as a slight delay in doing things can lead to the overall failure of the automated environment (Hartley, 2005). The awareness of this is of importance to the citizens of any smart environment and this invariably shapes their decision processes and instantaneous response to life situations (Nam & Pardo, 2011). It could be inferred that citizens of a smart environment are no time wasters, they are well organised and good planners.

## Ease of Doing Things

Since a smart environment is based and created upon planned and simulated events, proper planning of life activities is put in place to ease the manner of doing things (Nam & Pardo, 2011). Everything is well planned from traffic control to the least of everyday activity in such an environment. This is one of such advantages of living in a smart city and it goes beyond the environment but also has impacts on the citizenry as they live and dwell in the environment with ease.

## Waste Minimisation and Control

Waste minimisation is the process of reducing toxic materials from households to the environment. Smart city being a controlled environment with adequate planning, waste produced in such a city are well gathered, processed and used in generating power (Shooshtarian & Ridley, 2016). As citizens of the environment, indiscriminate refuse dumping is never an issue. Every individual recognises what constitute pollution and are conscious of where and how to dispose any toxic material generated in households without bringing neither harm to themselves nor their immediate environment.

### Good Transport Management

One of the major characteristics of a smart city is a well-automated transport system referred to as intelligent transport system (ITS) (Giffinger & Gudrun, 2010). This is a very complex system that uses information communication technology (ICT) technologies and services aimed at enhancing mobility and transportation. A better quality of life is what is gotten as a result of the introduction of ITS in smart cities. It has come about by the process of harnessing the combined power of computer processing, data management and modern communications to provide new and improved transportation services. All roads are well connected to a monitoring grid by the help of the internet (Thales, 2012). ITS involves road tolling services, safety cameras, smart ticketing systems for public transit, warning systems, incident detection, information services, city-wide synchronisation, E-ZPass and satellite navigation systems (UNRISD, 2012). The grid is made available to all road users with the aid of GPS which makes it easy to navigate the city.

Smart transportation helps in monitoring traffic and effective time management in the city (UNRISD, 2013). It improves accessibility economic performance, productivity, efficiency, and reduces waste, accidents and environmental damages. Smarter transportation means using all the available tools to provide the essential information and communications that balance the supply and demand of better networks. Some benefits accrued to citizens of smart city as seen in the quality of life they live are that they enjoy from the seamless services, while the authorities and administrators will reduce waste as network reliability and equilibrium is improved within the systems that are more integrated (Nam & Pardo, 2011). This also gives chance to stable market to service in the industries within the smart city.

## CONCLUSION

Smart technology is the backbone of any smart technology and the construction industry has been placed as a unifying entity to driving home the innovative thinking of the current advances made in this dispensation. In advanced nations of the world where smart technology has been tested and embraced, the quality of life of their citizens has been greatly been improved positively. Some of these improvements have been discussed in this write-up and some others include better standard of living, citizens' efficiency and effectiveness, interconnected environment (automation), increased productivity and by implication, increased life expectancy of the citizens.

## REFERENCES

Andamon, M. (2005). *Building climatology and thermal comfort.* Ph.D. thesis, University of Adelaide, Adelaide.

Giffinger, R., & Gudrun, H. (2010). Smart cities ranking: An effective instrument for the positioning of cities?. *Architecture, City and Environment*, *4*(12), 7–25.

Hartley, J. (2005). Innovation in governance and public services: Past and present. *Public Money and Management*, *25*(1), 27–34.

Nam, T., & Pardo, T. A. (2011). Smart city as urban innovation: Focusing on management policy, and context. In E. Estevez & M. Janssen (Ed.), *Proceeding of the 5th international conference on theory and practice of electronic governance* (pp. 185–194). New York, NY: ACM.

SDSN. (2013). *An action agenda for sustainable development.* Report for the Secretary-General, prepared by the Leadership Council of the Sustainable Development Solutions Network, New York.

Shooshtarian, S., & Ridley, I. (2016). Determination of acceptable thermal range in outdoor built environments by various methods. *Smart and Sustainable Built Environment*, *5*(4), 352–371.

Thales. (2012, July). SMART CITY, The interconnected city: Improving the quality of life of citizens. Retrieved from hhtp://www.thalesgroup.com

UNRISD. (2012). *Social dimensions of green economy.* New York, NY: United Nations Research Institute for Social Development.

UNRISD. (2013). *Emerging issues: Social drivers of sustainable development.* New York, NY: United Nations Research Institute for Social Development.

# 9

# SOCIALLY INCLUSIVE CITY: SOCIALLY INCLUSIVE AND ECONOMICALLY BENEFICIAL SMART CITIES


## ABSTRACT

*In the latest years of the twentieth century, information and communication technologies (ICT) and urbanisation are two major issues that are in egression. The progress in technology during the 1980s and 1990s majorly improved well-being in the urban centres. This encouraged development of urban centres, leading to the migration from rural areas to cities. This is with the motive that cities offer tonnes of opportunities in areas, such as social life, job, education, etc. Cities are the major pillars of economic and human activity. Furthermore, the demand for natural resources, energy and general resources for infrastructural developments are controlled by the nature and type of city. Therefore, it is expedient that urban centres strive to promote the sustainability of the environment, social unity and the standard of living of its inhabitants through effective support of economic competition and management of their developments. Therefore, in an effort to safeguard the health of the people and the condition of the earth from been ruined, the concept of 'Smart City' came into existence. In addition with the introduction of new technological concepts (majorly ICTs, the 'Smart City' concept has egresses as the pathway to accomplish more sustainable and efficient cities. This implies that such cities should not only accommodate the people with minimum health hazard but should be socially inclusive and economically beneficial to concerned stakeholders.*

**Keywords:** Energy efficiency; green infrastructure; Smart economy; Smart technology; sustainable development; sustainable urbanisation

## INTRODUCTION

According to the United Nations Environment Programme (UNEP, 2016) and the Sustainable Urbanization Policy 2016 brief, cities although occupies only 5% of the landmass of the earth, it consumes about 70% of the global energy supply and contributes about 70% of greenhouse gas emissions. Cities have also resulted in new increase in the requirement for land, food, water, building materials, waste management and pollution control measures. Because of these, cities are continuously pressurised to address congestion and environmental issues; increase efficiency and reduce cost, provide better quality services, improve service delivery and improve effectiveness and productivity, etc. All these among others encourage the development of what is described as a 'Smart City' (Huovila, Airaksinen, Pinto-Seppä, & Piira, 2017).

Simply described, smart cities are those that are able to solve problems associated with urban centres with proper consideration of the environment. Smart City concept have started gaining popularity right from the 1990s, and the concept implies a reaction that is driven by the community to mitigate the negative issues associated with urban centres, such as loss of open spaces, air pollution, overcrowding, traffic congestion and abrupt increment in cost of public facilities. However, the paradigm shift to resource efficient, climate resilient cities and low carbon initiatives through solutions that are innovative has a slow progress. United Nations (2014) propounds that the population of the world will increase by 32% between years 2015 and 2050, and that the urban population will increase by 63%. Furthermore, it predicted that by 2030, over 60% of the world population will reside in cities. Thus, smart solutions have the potency to address the challenges and surmount the barriers associated with cities are a welcomed development (Giffinger et al., 2007; Gonzales & Rossi, 2011; Pardo & Taewoo, 2011; UN-Habitat, 2011; United Nations, 2014, 2015;) . Therefore, it is not ambiguous to state that there exist a great motivation for innovative, user-friendly, efficient services and technologies especially in the aspect of transport, ICT and energy with incorporated and practical methods. Thus, the evolution of 'smart' solutions which apart from being greatly sustainable and efficient in one aspect, it also improves social well-being and generates economic prosperity. To attain these, it is expedient to properly coordinate the key players of the city and efficiently mobilise its resources through the utilisation of new technologies and advancement-oriented policies. Although, already there exist smart and innovative solutions for cities, however, the only challenge is that their application is below expectation. One good reason for this is that there is no objective proof to affirm that the effects of Smart City solutions will be visible if applied in other cities and contexts. In light of these, the popularity of the concept of 'Smart City' has become greater in international policies and scientific literatures over the last two decades. This might also be because the role played by cities in the economic and social areas worldwide cannot be ignored, and it also has much influence over the environment (Mori & Christodoulou, 2012). For a good understanding of the concept, it is noteworthy to assess it further.

## DESCRIPTIONS OF SMART CITIES

Cities contain what it takes to develop alliances that afford their residents great opportunities for development. In cities, there is tremendous and unique potential for economic growth, creativity, optimisation, exchanges and new solutions. Nevertheless, as they grow in size, a broad range of challenges that are difficult to handle are generated. The tendency of people to focus their attention on cities has resulted in both negative and positive consequences universally. Some of the negative consequences include more emissions of greenhouse gases and carbon dioxide, waste disposal problems, traffic jam, etc. Inequalities are also more pronounced in cities, and if these are not managed properly, the positive effects might be surmounted by the negative effects (Caragliu, Del Bo, & Nijkamp, 2011; Cocchia, 2014; Huovila et al., 2017; Monzon, 2015).

A key milestone to discovering the definition of Smart City is the equivocalness of meanings attached to the word smart and the label Smart City. Some examples of these equivocal meanings are: Knowledge City, Wired City, Digital City and Green City, etc. All these usually connect political, economic and sociocultural changes together with technology on information transformations. However, all these meanings are in certain way part of the Smart City fuzzy concept and can thus be regarded as a simple correlated topic of it (Hollands, 2008). Since it came into existence, the Smart City concept has emerged from the level of performing some particular projects to the level of global scheme execution to handle broad city problems (Caragliu et al., 2011; Cocchia, 2014; Monzon, 2015).

The term 'Smart City' encompasses many definitions across various understandings. However, none of these definitions have been accepted globally. However, the most popular terms used to describe the smartness of a city are

Digital City and Smart City. Smart cities presents a model for urban development that is based on the collective, human resource utilisation and technological capital required to advance the prosperity and development of urban centres (Angelidou, 2014; Mazza & Mavri, 2017).

## THE SMART CITY CONCEPT

Although there is a level of unanimity that the term Smart City signifies innovation in the management of city services and infrastructures, a universal definition for the term have not been posited yet. There are great numbers of definitions attempting to describe what a Smart City entails. However, in light of the major aspects that must be given sufficient attention by smart cities, two trends have been singled out. One of these trends is that a category of definitions emphasis an aspect of the urban settlement which consists of the ecological and technological areas. This category left out other events that occur within the city. The definitions by this category can be termed 'monotopic' in nature, and these carry the wrong notion about the ultimate aim of a Smart City. The ultimate aim of a Smart City is to furnish an innovative approach to urban management. In this approach, all areas are treated with the real life interconnection that occurs in the city. Advancement in one aspect of the urban ecosystem does mean that all the challenges will be conquered (Nam & Pardo, 2011).

The second trend is that another category of definitions are of the opinion that the major variant of the Smart City concept is the interconnection that exists between all its urban parts. The challenges associated with the institutional and social, infrastructure and urbanisation are intertwined, and this is shown in the Smart City concept. From these definitions, it will be observed that infrastructure is a cardinal segment of the Smart City, while the facilitator that brings it to reality is technology. However, what makes a city truly smart is the integration and connection of all its systems. Therefore, uniting these two trends of definitions, a Smart City concept can be put forward as an all-encompassing approach to city development and management. These definitions reflect a state of equilibrium among the social, technological and economic elements that constituent an urban ecosystem. They show an approach that utilises innovative technologies to handle urban challenges holistically, so as to redefine the relationship between the main urban players and the urban model (Monzon, 2015; Nam & Pardo, 2011). Some of the features of a Smart City are described in the Table 9.1. These include such items as energy,

**Table 9.1. Features of a Smart City.**

| Features of Smart City | Meaning |
|---|---|
| Flexible services | Flexibility in relation to social, cultural and economic conditions as services are offered with the aid of ICT |
| Energy | Energies are easily generated and supplied to the citizens without hassle |
| Planned transport system | Integrated transport system within the cities are well planned to bring convenience and time reduction in service offered |
| Connectivity | Activities carried out are well connected within a designed system to function well in payments, management, sustainability, delivery and so on |
| Health | Improvement in medical treatment and general services offered that relates to life and increasing green house for a standardised environment |
| Security | With the presence of enough technologies to power cameras and monitored systems, there is always an avenue for peace and reduced crime rates |
| Smart home | Smart homes in smart cities are controlled by the citizens, and this is made possible by the availability of automated platforms designed within and outside the city system |

flexible services, planned transport system, connectivity, health, security and smart homes.

## SMART CITY AS A SOCIALLY INCLUSIVE CITY

A Smart City is a connected city, and a connected city is socially inclusive. The entire system of a Smart City is based on technology. A Smart City is composed of interactive systems; and a great number of these systems are standardised and open, and they comprise the basic principles of a Smart City. A city that is not standardised and transparent can never be denoted as a Smart City. A Smart City is characterised by components such as high speed sensors, optical, wireless and wired networks in order to achieve intelligent transport systems, organisation of home and industrial networks and a smart power grid. Smart City empowers its citizens through the application of technology. One motive behind the Smart City concept is to improve sustainability, workability and liveability, and in order to achieve these, a broad range of components across the city are connected through the employment of the internet of things (IoT); and the technology of information and communications. Smart urban areas try to utilise innovation to put individuals first. In a period of associated innovations, our urban areas have the potential to be worked to react to our requirements and smoothen the way we live our lives. This smoother way will help all nationals, particularly those over a scope of ages and physical or psychological capacities. Envision a city where a man in a wheelchair or pushing a stroller can easily navigate a course to the neighbourhood stop, utilising control trims and keeping away from obstructions. Smart Cities improve the quality of its citizens' life by granting them access to the government, and smart resources that enhances investigation of civic problems with the aim of discovering solutions. A Smart City is one in which data can be obtained from a network that connects everything together, and this network improves the life of its citizens and enhances the communication between the government and the citizens (Bates, 2016; Korngold, Lemos, & Rohwer, 2017; Shichiyakh, Klyuchnikov, Balashova, & Novoselov, 2016).

A Smart City should be interconnected, intelligent and instrumented. This is conceivable when all the community and supervisory bodies running the city have brought order and control together. Connectivity is the core of a Smart City. The whole system of the city must have the capability to connect and communicate. It is also essential that those maintaining and monitoring the infrastructure should be able to access them remotely. In order to attain the financial and operational benefits the infrastructure offers, the citizens of the city should be able to communicate with the technology. Also, in order to develop new insights and innovations, it is expedient that developers and analysts are able to obtain efficient and real-time data as events unfolds. For example, those controlling traffic should be able to obtain real-time data on the nature of the traffic on the roads, the number of vehicles, real-time images, etc., so as to discharge their duties efficiently without leaving their offices (Aeris, 2016).

If inclusion and equity are not properly considered and incorporated into the planning of Smart Cities, it could increase economic segregation and social injustices such as ageism and discrimination. Bates (2016) opines that it is unfortunate that some governments all over the planet earth are spending a lot of money to transform their cities into a Smart City without giving appropriate consideration to the issues relating to inclusion and equity. A proper consideration and incorporation of strategies relating to inclusion and equity will ensure all residents including those with disabilities and those that have advanced in age, have equal access to Smart City services. Where the Smart City services are not accessible, it results in exclusion, inequality and isolation of the citizens for which they were initially designed, especially those with disabilities. Therefore a city that lacks accessibility is wrong to be considered as a Smart City; rather it is just a non-inclusive city. A city that is connected by a network of technology is not accessible to its citizens is not a Smart City.

## SMART CITY AS AN ECONOMICALLY BENEFICIAL CITY

A Smart City when viewed through the lens of social and economic aspects is a city that ensures optimisation of the allocation and utilisation of resources through the continuous observation of vital infrastructures, such as tunnels, subways, railways, highways, bridges, ports, communications, airports, power supply, water supply, etc. (Shichiyakh et al., 2016). Therefore, one of the main goals of a Smart City is to harness technology and enable the development of the local environment for the purpose of promoting economic growth and improving the standard of living of the people. Transforming a city into a smart one or creating a Smart City is not a cheap enterprise. But there are several means to save costs including putting infrastructures that are already in existence into use. For example, in some cities, front of buildings, streetlight columns and CCTV columns are being employed to extend wireless networks, 3G and 4G network availability. All these already existing infrastructures can provide simpler and less expensive means to IoT and mobile operators to improve and broaden their network coverage. IoT is a core aspect of Smart City; it promotes connectivity, by integrating different devices like mobile devices, sensors, etc., and making it possible for them to communicate with each other with little human input. IoT is enhancing the improvement of cities by making available avenue for maximising the use of facilities and resources that are limited in supply while at the same time providing a better living condition for everyone. To form the networks required in a Smart City system, the public can also go into partnership with the commercial entities (Aeris, 2016; Smart Home Energy, 2017).

A Smart City creates collaborations and enhances efficiencies in whatever way possible. It promotes cross marketing of councils and infrastructures. These can result in cost saving and eliminate disruptions and improve the revenues obtained from investments. For example, a company might want to lay water pipes, several mobile networks might one to lay their optical fibre cables, all these can collaborate together and join resources to dig the trench required to bury their pipes and cables. This will be cheaper in cost that each company digging up their own trench. The infrastructure and technology in a city that is truly smart should be put into maximum use with the correct information on what it is used for, and how often it is being used. Technology makes it possible to get this information, together with the ones relating to: When it is used? How it is operated? What the cost of operation? and What the maintenance cost is like? When the right information is available, it is employed in creating a plan that can cover up to a period of five years. Once this plan has been formulated, proper and well informed decisions can be made on new investment.

## CONCLUSION

Transforming a city into a smart one or creating a Smart City is not a cheap enterprise; however, with the cooperation of all the city stakeholders, the realisation of a Smart City is not something that is unachievable. Smart City has many benefits towards its citizens as well as to the economy of the city. It improves the living standard of its current citizens and that of its future generation. Since it is self-sustaining, the cost of maintenance and control will be within a manageable range. The city also has several advantages in relation to the environment. Among these is the reduction of greenhouse gases to the atmosphere among others. Therefore, the Smart City concept is a welcomed innovation and every city of the world is encouraged to strive to achieve its principles for its overall improvement.

## REFERENCES

Aeris. (2016, October 6). A smart city is a truly connected city. Retrieved from http://www.aeris.com/news-post/smart-city-truly-connected-city/. Accessed on November 22, 2017.

Angelidou, M. (2014). *Smart City Policies: A spatial approach*. Thessaloniki: Aristotle University of Thessaloniki.

Bates, D. (2016, August 16). A smart city is a connected city, a connected city is an inclusive city. Retrieved from https://www.linkedin.com/pulse/smart-city-connected-inclusive-darren-bates. Accessed on November 13, 2017.

Caragliu, A., Del Bo, C., & Nijkamp, P. (2011). Smart cities in Europe. *Journal of Urban Technology*, *18*(2), 65–82.

Cocchia, A. (2014). *Smart and digital city: A systematic literature review*. Geneva: Springer International Publishing.

Giffinger, R., Fertner, C., Kramar, H., Kalasek, R., Pichler-Milanovic, N., & Meijers, E. (2007). Smart cities – Ranking of European medium-sized cities

Final Report. Centre of Regional Science, Vienna, UT. Retrieved from www.smart-cities.eu. Accessed on October 20, 2017.

Gonzales, J. A., & Rossi, A. (2011). New trends for smart cities, open innovation mechanism in smart cities. European Commission with the ICT Policy Support Programme. Retrieved from http://ec.europa.eu/information_society/apps/projects/logos/6/270896/080/deliverables/001_D2221NewtrendsforSmartCities.pdf

Hollands, R. (2008). Will the Real Smart City Please Stand Up? *Analysis of Urban Change, Theory, Action*, *12*(3), 303–320.

Huovila, A., Airaksinen, M., Pinto-Seppä, I., & Piira, K. (2017). Citykeys smart city performance measurement system. *International Journal for Housing Science and Its Applications*, *41*(2), 113–125.

Korngold, D., Lemos, M., & Rohwer, M. (2017). Smart cities for all: A vision for an inclusive, accessible urban future. *BSR*. Retrieved from http://smartcities4all.org/wp-content/uploads/2017/06/Smart-Cities-for-All-A-Vision-for-an-Inclusive-Accessible-Urban-Future...-min.pdf. Accessed on November 22, 2017.

Mazza, P. I., & Mavri, M. (2017). The concept of Smart Cities; A literature review and a proposed framework for analyzing and enriching dimensions of the "smartness" of a city. Retrieved from http://asrdlf2017.com/asrdlf2017_com/inc/resumes/323.pdf. Accessed on October 22, 2017.

Monzon, A. (2015). Smart cities concept and challenges: Bases for the assessment of smart city projects. In *Smart cities, Green Technologies, and Intelligent Transport systems, 4th international conference, SMARTGREENS 2015 and 1st International conference*, Lisbon.

Mori, K., & Christodoulou, A. (2012). Review of sustainability indices and indicators: Towards a New City, Sustainability Index (CSI). *Environmental Impact Assessment Review*, *32*(1), 94–106.

Nam, T., & Pardo, T. A. (2011). Smart city as urban innovation: Focusing on management policy, and context. In E. Estevez & M. Janssen (Eds.), Proceeding of the 5th *international conference on theory and practice of electronic governance* (pp. 185–194). New York, NY: ACM.

Pardo, T., & Taewoo, N. (2011). Conceptualizing smart city with dimensions of technology, people, and institutions. In *Proceedings of the 12th annual international conference on digital government research*, New York, NY (pp. 282–291).

Shichiyakh, R. A., Klyuchnikov, D. A., Balashova, S. P., & Novoselov, S. N. (2016). Smart city as the basic construct of the socio-economic development of territories. *International Journal of Economics and Financial Issues*, 6(1), 157–162.

Smart Home Energy. (2017). What is a “Smart Home”? Retrieved from http://smarthomeenergy.co.uk/what-smart-home. Accessed on December 4, 2017.

UNEP. (2016). Cities and climate change. Retrieved from http://www.unep.org/resourceefficiency/Policy/ResourceEfficientCities/FocusAreas/CitiesandClimateChange/tabid/101665/Default.aspx. Assessed on February 11, 2016.

UN-Habitat. (2011). *Cities and climate change: Global report on human settlements*. London: Human Settlements Programme, United Nations.

United Nations. (2014). World urbanization prospectes. 2014 Revision: Highlights.

United Nations. (2015). World population prospectes. 2015 Revision: Key findings and advance tables.

# PART 6

# ENHANCING SMART CITIES FOR SUSTAINABLE DEVELOPMENT

# 10

# DRIVERS OF SMART CITIES


## ABSTRACT

*Smart cities over the years is fast growing on people. Citizens and stakeholders that were defiant to its adoption are beginning to see the reasons for it. Due to one reason or the other, many of the stakeholders and the citizens were reluctant in seeing the vision in the smart city system. Some of these factors are expressed in the drivers and challenges faced in enhancing from a city to smart city. Along with these, measures and benefits that relate with smart city has helped in social and general awareness of what it represents and what stands to be gained if fully adopted. And this has helped in overall information available on smart city. The concluding part of the chapter gives a summary of the importance in addressing these drivers.*



**Keywords:** Decision making; digital city; smart city development; smart city drivers sustainability; sustainable development


## INTRODUCTION

'Smart city' is gaining more popularity in international policies and scientific literature for decades. The reason for its popularity is not unconnected to cities rendering a core contribution to environmental, economic and social prospect worldwide. The objective of this study is to provide an enlightenment on the drivers of smart city. The study starts with explanation of smart city in relation to construction development and then proceeds with a brief explanation of it. It also highlights and explains explicitly the drivers of smart city. The study comes to a close with some of the benefits derived from smart city development.

## BRIEF EXPLANATION OF SMART CITY

Smart city simply put is the integration of smartrness into the concepts of city. This can be further described as the introduction of several technolological advanced technologies into constructing a city for the benefits of all. Even though the concept of smart city has been propounded for ages, it is however not being fully implemented in most cities. This is due to some challenges that revolves around perception and awareness of what it represents and the ways it is going to affect the running of activities in such city where it is adopted.

In considering the settings of smart city along with the functionality of a particular existing city, there is an integration of principles that works together to function systematically. One of such systems is the communication between the parties involved in setting up and decision making. These parties are majorly the construction stakeholders in charge of the smart city concept and the citizens of the proposed city. Furthermore, implementing information friendly interface within the urban spaces adds more understanding to what the smart city tends to offer all parties involved when fully operational.

Smart cities tackle most of the challenges faced today. Some of which are global change, scarcity of resources, pollution and so on. Since the implementation of smart city is not peculiar to individuals alone, it is necessary to put in place measures that will assist the government in making policies that are directly involved in making the possibility of smart city a reality especially in most developing countries. In studies carried out by Alawadhi et al. (2012), Ballas (2013) and Vito, Umberto, and Rosa (2015), the interest of government and concerned parties about the sustainability possibilities in smart city was established and that they are working towards implementing the concept in most cities as it is accepted to bring growth in all areas of the city's economy.

## DRIVERS OF SMART CITY

The forces shaping the smart city market are complex and multi-faceted. Below are five key underlying drivers:

(a) Waste not, want not.

(b) Knowledge is power.

(c) Citizen empowerment and engagement.

(d) Balancing the budget.

(e) Low risk living.

(a) *Waste not, want not*: cities are held back by the availability of energy, clean water, land and other key resources. Based on the increase of urban residents on daily basis, urban areas as a matter of urgency, need to cut back waste to ensure there are enough resources in circulation and avoid civil unrest. Road space needs to be efficiently allocated, electricity used judiciously and water leaks plugged. Data available can be accessed and analysed in order to assist in allocating resources and managing wastes used by the citizens.

(b) *Knowledge is power:* the ever increasing population of the urban areas is putting a lot of pressure in tracking and monitoring activities in most urban areas. It is quite difficult to control these activities and monitor them through mechanisms operated manually, such as site visits, town hall meetings and conventional complaints procedures. Rather than scrambling resources to react to problems retrospectively, municipalities realise that they need to become more proactive and productive. To that end, mayors are beginning to use connected sensors as their eyes and ears.

(c) *Citizen empowerment and engagement:* the benefits in the adoption of smart city will reduce challenges that are faced directly or indirectly when living in urban areas. As earlier discussed in defining smart city, communication and passage of information forms the basic towards the citizens' acceptance of the concept. This will offer them choices in the first place and the power to making them at the long run. For example, when citizens have access to applications on their gadgets and trucks, it could alert them of possible blockage on a particular route when driving and they can make decision in taking another route suggested by the intelligence offered by the mechanics controlling the application. Furthermore, possible life threatening situations can be averted when there is a passage of information through installed or available devices that will assist the citizens in having a better quality of life in peace and little or no stress at all. Also, through cameras installed everywhere, crimes can be easily detected and avoided. All these and more are ways of empowering and engaging the populace towards smart city development.

(d) *Balancing the budget:* there is no better way to accountability than being monitored in an algorithm that offers solutions to possible under or over costing. Through this means, costs are reduced to the barest minimum while quality is obtained at the same time in satisfaction and revenue. Example of this can be noted in analysing the cost and value of a supposed construction project through artificial intelligence software. Value is created within the shortest duration and execution is prompt within a budgeted contract.

(e) *Low risk living:* when the system is controlled and well monitored, life threatening situations are easily averted. People live in cities where many lives are at risk of danger because of challenges presented within the city system, smart city on the other hand brings solutions to these problems. Some of the problems faced include floods, earthquakes, traffic congestion, pollutions and so on. These problems are controlled through differently installed cameras and sensors across the nooks and crannies of the smart city to alarm the authorities and citizens of impeding dangers before they occur. Data received are swiftly analysed and inferential solutions are suggested within the quickest time possible.

In addition, drivers of smart city can also be perceived in connection with the following concerns:

1. Energy and the environment

2. Economy

3. Mobility

4. Society

5. Governance

## Energy and the Environment

The greater the amount of energy released into the environment, the greater it affects the environment and everything in it. Due to overpopulation in most cities, controlling energy usage is difficult and a challenging one at that. Smart supplies, metres and channels are important in the transfer and distribution of energy as well as storage within a controlled environment. Even though most of the attention is always on the technological aspect of a smart city, the energy present in it should be as important as other considerations. Through intelligent supply and control channels, transparency is ensured and sanity maintained within an already established environment.

### Economy

Arguably the most benefitted aspect of smart city is the economy growth. The concept offers growth in several factors that include education, research, technology, entrepreneurship, production, marketing, innovation, delivery and so on. These smart economies are enhanced profoundly through already linked networks. The use of information technology into running operations brings ease throughout the economic process from the goods and services rendered to when it gets to the final consumers.

### Mobility

Accessibility is never an issue in a smart system. Friendly users and environmentally friendly cars are manufactured in the system to provide ease and comfort. With the provision and availability of modern transport systems, traffic is reduced and swiftness gained which transmits to economy growth. Smart mobility gives access to implementation of plans. For example, the fire service can get to a place razed with fire quicker when accessibility is ensured on the roads.

### Society

Quality of life of the citizens is increased in a smart system. This is however not made possible only through technical innovations. The societal aspect of increase must focus on improving education, health, transport, culture, safety, power supply, housing and social interactions. The availability of these will bring out the best out of the people living in such smart city. Networks are also easily connected within the society and better interactions will propel greatness in a functional society.

### Governance

When a society is governed in a smart environment by smart government officials, the creativeness that will be experienced in such environment is never going to be matched. One of the ways of achieving this is encouraging the citizens to cooperate with themselves towards enhancing the economy of the city. The government promotes this interaction by making available provisions in the system that allows for self-discovery and expression where citizens that can feel to be an integral part of the city system. Furthermore, provisions should also come in forms of research, grant, business platforms, data accessibility, etc. Transparency is expected from every government official in a smart city system.

## MEASURES OF SMART CITY PERFORMANCE

The effectiveness and efficiency of the following indicators speak more volume on positive or good performance of smart city as opined by Vito et al., (2015):

1. Amount spent publicly in research and development.
2. Percentage of population with secondary school level.
3. Individual level of computer skill.
4. Public expenditure on education.
5. Willingness to partake in long learning process.
6. Available of tertiary institutions and research centres.
7. Factors in accessing the internet.
8. Perception of the individuals on digital economy.
9. Energy reduction strategy.
10. Provisions and efficiencies in the usage of electricity.
11. Water usage.
12. Green areas available.
13. Energy consumption in relation to gas emitted.
14. Maintaining tranquillity through policies.
15. Level of waste recycled.
16. Recreation available and sport.
17. Accessibility to public libraries.

18. Leisure in visiting amusement parks.
19. Creating time for the theatre and cinema.
20. Willingness to be creative.
21. Transparency exhibited by the government.
22. Resources available for sustainable development.
23. Education and relative facilities.
24. Health status and survival.
25. Sustainable and environmentally friendly transport system.
26. Availability of pedestrian channels.
27. Lanes that are circle in nature.
28. Solid municipal waste produced.
29. Political view, fuel and strategies.
30. Presence of information communication technology enabled infrastructures.
31. Flexibility in the labour market.
32. City population in gross domestic product per count.
33. Rate of unemployment.t
34. Ability to speak foreign languages.
35. Patent applications per inhabitant.

## BENEFITS OF SMART CITY TO THE CITIZENS

The following are benefits of smart city:

1. It paves way for a safer, cleaner and more efficient urban areas.
2. It enhances the efficiency of traffic infrastructure, and to increase the safety and convenience of users.
3. It provides citizens with a safer living environment.
4. Information needed to mitigate against emergent and disastrous situation are made available such as earthquake, flood, etc.

5. It provides a platform to measure excessive weather and atmospheric condition.
6. Information regarding public administration, processes of civil affairs are provided to the citizens through mobile devices for increase and enhancement of efficiency of operations, and citizen satisfaction respectively.
7. It enhances integrated facility management (Sang, Heeseo, HeeAh, Jongbok, & Donju, 2016).

## CONCLUSIONS

The fact that urban settlement are becoming overcrowded and highly congested necessitates the development of 'smart city' and makes it inevitable in this modern era. This study provided enlightenment on some core drivers of smart city which if properly and carefully addressed and evaluated would provide citizens with a safer living environment, pave way for cleaner and more efficient urban area and even provide platform to measure excessive atmospheric weather condition. An in-depth analysis of the literature revealed that the meaning of a smart city as a multi-faceted concepts. Smart cities are now including qualities of people and communities as well as its drivers. Some elements of smart cities are expressed in monitored, functioning,transportation and traffic systems, adequate and quality water supply systems, efficient waste management systems, power plant, information system, schools, hospitals and other community programmes and services. For a city to be regarded as a smart city , some drivers such as low risk living; a well-established sustainable pillars; waste not, want not concept; knowledge as power driven the smart city's concept; balancing the budgets employed for the project construction; and citizen empowerment and engagement must be the core driven force of such city. This is done by engaging the local contents of the immediate environment such as the local raw materials, local labour, local technology and local methods of construction and so on into the intended smart city development.

## REFERENCES

Alawadhi, S., Aldama-Nalda, A., Chourabi, H., Gil-Garcia, J. R., Leung, S., Mellouli, S., ... Walker, S. (2012). Building understanding of smart city initiatives. *Lecture Notes in Computer Science*, *7443*, 40–53.

Ballas, D. (2013). What makes a 'happy city'?. *Cities in International Journal of Urban Policy and Planning*, *32*(1), 39–50. http://dx.doi.org/10.1016/j.cities.2013.04.009

Sang, K. L., Heeseo, R. K., HeeAh, C., Jongbok, K., & Donju, L. (2016). International case studies of smart cities Songdo, Republic of Korea. IDB Publication, North Korea. Retrieved from https://www.kdevelopedia.org

Vito, A., Umberto, B., & Rosa, M. D. (2015). Smart cities: Definitions, dimensions, performance, and initiatives. *Journal of Urban Technology*, *22*(1), 3–21. http://dx.doi.org/10.1080/10630732.2014.942092

# 11

# SMART CITY DIMENSIONS


## ABSTRACT

*The enhancement of cities can be affirmed when there is a transformation in the functions it is used to perform to ones that are just experienced in all newness and effectiveness. A city enhanced in all smartness and dimensions can always perform better when quality of life is targeted during and after a designed project. These dimensions come in the form of smart economy, smart transportation, smart environment, smart individual, smart living and good governance. Other aspects of the chapter include cities and smart cities, formation of smart cities, idea of smart city and barriers to smart city development. All these work together to function together in understanding and maintaining a regulated smart city supply chain in the construction industry.*



**Keywords:** City performance; city transformation; construction industry; planning; smart administration; Sustainability


## INTRODUCTION

### Cities

Munford (2007) defines city as theatre of social action and everything else such as education, art, politics and commerce. A city is referred to as being smart when human, social resources, transport, communication and infrastructure are being invested upon to encourage sustainability, development in economy and life quality. It encompasses the interaction between factors in assets and capital towards human's satisfaction (Caragliu, Del Bo, & Nijkamp, 2011; Schaffers et al., 2011). Although, researches by Shen, Jorge Ochoa, Shah, and Zhang (2011) and Tegua, D'Auria, and Bifulco (2015) oppose the practicality of a city to function as smart city especially when there are several terminologies used by various researchers.

### Smart City

Smart cities entail constructions with smart devices. It is commonly known that the idea of brain lightning is to save energy. However, this brain itself is founded on technology which may not engage the inhabitants. The inhabitants only need to be aware in order to be able to utilise the technology installed perfectly in terms of the digital, physical and human scheme in the latest environs so as to deliver a supportable, successful and better future for all citizens.

All cities differs in history, culture, economy, politics and social life. The nature of business, religion and technology operation in each city makes it unique. Citizens represent the residents, tourists, industries and customers of a city. The United Kingdom strategy technology board focusses on the digital, physical and human world rather than visualising the future of the city.

## FORMATION OF SMART CITIES

Nevertheless smart city is known to be the ability of a city focussing on various aspects. The term is not commonly used in three-dimensional planning; various aspects can be identified on consistent amplification.

In relative to jobs, smart city can be described to be smart industry. Smart city also implies to education, information communication and technology. Smart city refers to the relationship between the government admin and its inhabitants/citizens. Smart administration is an act of good governance through establishment of communication channels to the citizens. Furthermore, smart city qualifies the use of contemporary technology in municipal life. Smart mobility involves modern transport technologies and logistics as well as a new system transport that improves the urban transportation of mobilising citizens.

Landscape, green house, security and sustainable energy are all part of smart city. Smart city can be grouped into six characteristics. A smart city with its effective system of communication and substantial information should be a ground to alert all manners of environmental challenges or problems. A city performance depends not only on the available natural resources but on the communication links, information standard and social frame.

The six characteristics of smart city include economy, mobility, environment, people, living and governance. Smart mobility has to do with transportation system; smart environment includes landscape, infrastructure and surrounding resources; smart people refers to the inhabitants; smart living involves standard of living; and smart governance the system of ruling. Fig. 11.1 highlights good governance, smart living, smart economy, smart individual, smart transportation and smart environment as chain of dimension in smart city. There is a connection among the variables that makes up the chain for effective smart city system.

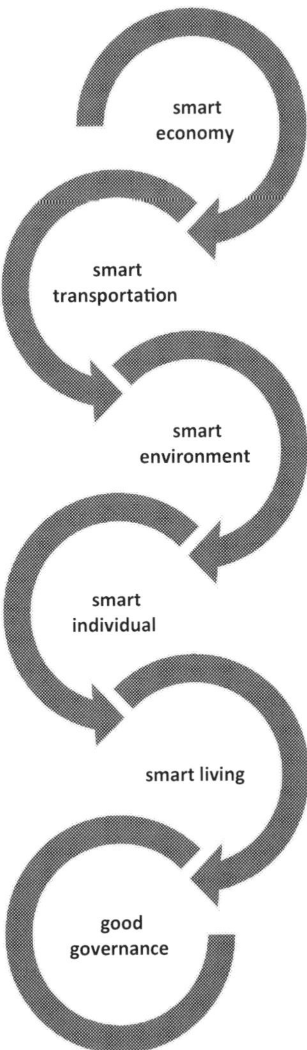


**Fig. 11.1. Smart City Chain of Dimension.**

### Smart Economy

(Competitiveness)

1. Labor market flexibility.
2. Productivity.
3. Innovative spirit.
4. Transforming ability.
5. Entrepreneurship.
6. Economic image and trademarks.
7. International relationship.

### Smart Transportation

(Transportation and information and communication technology, ICT)

1. Access to international system.
2. New development and maintenance of easy transport system.
3. Access to local system.
4. Availability of information computer technology.

### Smart Environment

(The available natural resources)

1. Sustainable resource management.
2. Attraction of natural state of affairs.
3. Protection of the environment against pollution.
4. General protection of the environment.

### Smart Individuals

(Societal and human capital)

1. Empathy to lifespan learning.
2. Social and indigenous variety.

3. Qualification level.

4. Involvement in municipal life.

5. Inventiveness.

6. Flexibility.

7. Cosmopolitanism/open mindedness.

## Good Governance

(Involvement)

1. Involvement in decision making.

2. Social amenities and municipal life.

3. Government transparency.

4. Political approaches and perceptions.

## Smart Living

(The quality of life)

1. Traditional amenities.

2. Health situations and fitness.

3. Safety of inhabitants.

4. Quality of shelter.

5. Education services.

6. Tourism.

7. Societal structure.

The above characteristics forms a framework for indicating the evaluation of the performance of a city as to decide if it is a smart city. Smart city makes use of information and computer technology in order to effectively make judicious use of the natural resources, which brings about cost reduction, improved quality of life, perfect service delivery and saves energy.

The European Commission Award Communication and Smart Cities Community European Innovation enters into partnership. This partnership is to draw the resources or amenities to enhance the combination of transport, energy and ICT in cities. And through this, a smart city network and the people development has been recognised. On the regular meetings, technology developers are brought together, there is always a review in the presence of financial managers and policy makers from the union with a view to access the viability of smart cities across the country.

## IDEA OF SMART CITY

Half of a country population dwell in cities. Most developed countries policy administrators are faced with the challenge of smart governance especially in social terms like education, technology and resources. The sustainability of smart city depends on the ability to reduce noise, reduce energy use, reduce pollution in the environment and provide greener urban environment.

The idea of this smart city explodes regularly in the urban development situation. The situation adds sweet savour to the environment, meaning that there is no specific definition of smart city. The definitions, meaning comes from different stakeholders, individuals and it varies. The impression created is that it is a digital city, anything can be created within the concept of smart city through inhabitants activities. Activities such as creating power grids around power plants and the routes and schedules are been scheduled by others on the public's behalf as well as well-built shopping malls in place of retail marketing. Information and communication have been greatly developed to enhance public research system. The implementation of those points said above is referred to as smart. The changes to smart can only be attained through ICT, service providers and end users are made impossible through this link. Internet shopping has eaten into local environment thereby taking over the roles of shopping plazas and market stores changing the end delivery to citizens. The advance ICT has brought about high responsiveness to consumers need. Due to this development, the quality of life and standard of living have been improved. The services can be accessed everywhere at any time.

## BARRIERS TO SMART CITY DEVELOPMENT

The barriers to smart city development can be identified as follows:

1. Complexity of smart city system.

2. Economic barriers.

3. Technological barriers.

4. Social barriers.

5. Unclear vision.

6. Information and awareness.

7. Governance and coordination barriers.

8. Legal and regulatory.

9. Financial barriers.

## Complexity of Smart City System

Smart city comprises of many components. These components make it complex as it involves barriers like integration and convergence issues, administrative and technology maturity differences, standardisation, open data, private and security issues and integration and convergence issues amongst others.

Cities focus more on technology investments on adorning energy management, water supply and transport management. The energy management is to reduce the use of energy, ensure constant water supply into all cities and reduce traffic congestion.

The convergence issue needs be considered so as to interchange information between persons, machines to machines, people and machine and vice versa. A genuine smart city would incorporate technology into infrastructure making the city to perform single system operation and also need to cut across national, international and local structures. It includes wireless technologies.

A genuine smart city would incorporate technology into infrastructure making the city to perform single system operation and also need to cut across national, international and local structures. It includes wireless technologies. Administrative and technological advancement, in the formation of smart city, must be considered in the process of developing numerous urban cities. They produce enormous institutions such as health, education, social and economic development and so on that are of different benefits to citizens within the local, national and foreign administrative infrastructures. The effects of the differences in administrative and maturity delay the ability of developing smart city. It includes problem of coordination of high number of associates and authorities, lack of good collaboration and recognition among associates, poor public participation and poor institutions or mechanisms to distribute information, time consuming and difficult processes for approval of project activities.

Standardisation is obviously a crucial assignment affecting the software that connects clients with database implementation, ensuring transparency and also the compatibility of products and services across various territories.

Open data in developing smart city requires logical approach to technology advancement. Open data in developing smart city requires logical approach to technology advancement. This is crucial in the formation of urban centres, businesses and inhabitants resorts. Open data is also a prerequisite in smart Cities electronic governance. It should be easily accessible throughout a nation, this will enable developers to have basis to act upon maps, information, timetables, data, etc.

The confidentiality in privacy and security should be directed towards building the confidence of new developers and end users in further technologies so as to facilitate the acceptance of smart city. For people to embrace smart city they must be sure their personal data are safe.

## Economic Barriers

There are certain needs in developing infrastructural and intelligent systems; they are finance and infrastructural problems. The question of funding investments, what yield and how long is asked. When it comes to economic challenges, most mentioned problems here are financial and infrastructural. There is a need for smart city to be set in current infrastructures such as transport, buildings, power plants, etc. which might agree with sustainability. There is a need for smart city to be set in current infrastructures such as transport, buildings, power plants, etc. which might agree with sustainability. Also, in business model delivery of smart services and finance modernism, challenge such as obtaining financial plan for large scale projects are distinctive, since the exploitation of high technology network is required to achieve the city. In countries like Europe and United States, investment funds are rare, to invest in new technologies, cities will need to take an innovative step in deriving operating model, business model and finance model.

## Technological Barriers

Technological barriers include deficiency in demonstrated and confirmed results and models, inadequate skilful and well trained personnel, improper planning and lack of well-defined method. Barriers of information communication technologies include inadequate knowledge regarding security, privacy and cost of implementation, accessible and compactible software, application of software, threats from hackers, viruses, etc.

## Social Barriers

Social barriers include disinterest, lack of values and interest in energy optimisation measurements and low recognition of different projects and technologies. Involvement of end users: the cooperation of citizens is crucial in accepting new styles of delivering basic service. The problem of how to motivate, enlighten end users is being faced.

Some cities adopt a narrow-minded view of value in economic terms. The city lacks the abundance and multiplicity of life. The problems come in when it is difficult to derive a model for measuring and communicating value that booms with inhabitants and empowers politicians to express how to enrich life in diverse manner.

### *Unclear Vision*

It is not visible to the public how smart technologies will resolve everyday activities problem. The description of technology may not be clear and can blind the impact of technology.

### *Information and Awareness*

This includes insufficient information on the part of potential users and consumers and lack of awareness among authorities. Awareness of the general public on smart city: most successful cities have not overcome this barrier, most citizens of a particular smart city may not be aware that the city was designed through the initiative of city developers.

## Governance and Coordination Barriers

Inadequate support from the government as a result of having fear of losing power and potential resistance from the inhabitants of the city. The formation of a city is a long process, it can be time consuming which can prevent inventive, under resourced companies from partaking in smart city formation. The ICT that improves, promotes or encourages governance is referred to smart governance. It requires gathering of people, technologies, norms, culture, resources, data, etc. and relates to encourage the activities of governing city. The collaboration of public/private partnership enhances the good governance.

### *Legal and Regulatory*

The barrier of smart city formation can also be traceable to inadequate regulations for technologies that are new, unstable rules, likewise regulations that are not effective and policies that do not support innovative technologies.

## FINANCIAL BARRIERS

In developing smart city, if the cost of designing, procuring or obtaining material, construction and installation is high, it will affect the formation of the city and also when there is inadequate financial support or low funds available for project activities. Crisis in economy and risk can also be a barrier to the formation of city.

## SOLUTIONS TO SMART CITY DEVELOPMENT BARRIERS

The various barriers of developing smart city have been identified above. Generally, all these barriers are grouped into public and private, the references for both sectors range majorly across complexity, social, technical, economical and governance barriers.

## PUBLIC SECTOR REFERENCES

### To Overcome Complexity Barriers

The need to share knowledge deliberately between government and citizens, develop method in spreading smart city services, dependence on the level of technology development, understanding of citizens and government potential services with ICT, benchmarking and regulation of projects in order to achieve a healthy society to promote ICT services sealed to inhabitants way of living. Regulation of positive project performance and enhancing the adoption of the best method. Expansion of best practices through establishment of legal foundation.

### To Overcome Economic Barriers

One of the ways to overcome the economic barrier in developing smart city is to develop latest service models and spread the performance in order to increase demands for new technologies in the public.

### To Overcome Technological Barriers

The services of the public can be improved through advancement or progressive ICT, increment of ICT aptitude and smart devices. Improvement in the network system and service consumer acceptance. The availability of all these thing in excess will promote the establishment of smart cities and will also meet the expectation of citizens' future needs.

### To Overcome Social Barriers

To overcome social barriers, more values need be created through sustainable smart green. This engages the services of citizens and change their attitude through robust incentive system. Government should be transparent and needs to source for crowd, expanding and discovering various service territories (utilities, transportation and healthcare).

### To Overcome Governance Barriers

Government should contribute to creating initial market setting for e-governance. The method of governing smart city should be updated in relative to the large potential of projects. This can be achieved by setting up the programmes with the right competencies. Developing smart city involves large processes and dedicated organisations, good government policies and so on.

## PRIVATE SECTOR REFERENCES

### To Overcome Complexity Barriers

Partnering with government agencies, creation of ecosystem for improvement and investments through private–public collaboration, incorporating planning are ways to overcome complexity barriers.

### To Overcome Economic Barriers

In order to overcome the economic barriers in private sector, there should be business model inventions for a strategic and investment approach to ICT.

### To Overcome Technological Barriers

Overcoming technological barrier can be as a result of investing in technology to create value for latest service invention, developing much more intelligence technical product to support various services.

### To Overcome Social Barriers

Expressing the vision of smart city with much clarity using metrics. Involving knowledgeable and experience personnel for proper scaling of projects that are larger.

### To Overcome Governance Barriers

There is need to concentrate on business model invention as a reference to scaling through the barriers of economic and governance. This will flourish the digital economy if implemented. Leaders should undergo strategic planning procedure to focus on the economy, the update of personal data contribute to the monitoring of the environment of the city, for citizens to be able to register their information they must be aware of the safety of their information.

## CONCLUSION

A smart city is a city that performs excellently, built on the combination of endowed resources and activities of citizens. Through intelligent ICT, strategic planning process smart city is established. The barriers to smart city development discussed earlier are as follows: complexity of smart city system, economic barriers, technological barriers, social barriers, unclear vision, information and awareness, governance and coordination barriers, legal and regulatory and financial barriers. Certain references to providing solution to these problems are grouped into the private and public sectors of the economy.

## REFERENCES

Caragliu, A., Del Bo, C., & Nijkamp, P. (2011). Smart cities in Europe. *Journal of Urban Technology*, *18*, 65–82. doi:10.1080/10630732.2011.601117

Munford, L. (2007). Urbanism in the archaeological record: What is a city?. Retrieved from https://www.brown.edu/Departments/Joukowsky_Institute/courses/urbanism/3981.html

Schaffers, H., Komninos, N., Pallot, M., Trousse, B., Nilsson, M., & Olivera, A. (2011). Smart cities and the future internet: Towards cooperation frameworks for open innovation. *The Future Internet*, 66(56), 431–446.

Shen, L. Y., Jorge Ochoa, J., Shah, M. N., & Zhang, X. (2011). The application of urban sustainability indicators – A comparison between various practices. *Habitat International*, *35*(1), 17–29.

Tegua, M., D'Auria, A., & Bifulco, F. (2015). Comparing research streams on smart city and sustainable city. *China USA Business Review*, *14*(4), 203–215.

# 12

# CHALLENGES IN SMART CITIES DEVELOPMENT

## ABSTRACT

*In discussing the developments attached to smart city in terms of how it affects life and the environment, several factors contribute one way or the other towards the development. Smart city development comes with its advantages that can be experienced within and outside the construction environment, the challenges faced in putting in place smart city are enormous in relation to the nature and type of smart city propounded. These challenges are discussed extensively in information technology (IT) infrastructure, security and privacy, big data management, cost, efficiency, availability and scalability, social adaption and application development. Solutions must be found to these challenges for the construction industry to be able to convince individuals concerned with giving directives and policies regarding city development.*

**Keywords:** Smart city challenges; smart city cost; smart city development; smart infrastructure; smart policy and economy; social adoption

## INTRODUCTION

The quest to provide improved quality of life to citizen is what brought about the concept termed smart city. This is under a key idea of integrating information system service to provide public services to citizen efficiently. Some of these services include healthcare, education, transportation, power grid, etc.

These expectations invoke massive challenges in the efficiency and realisation of development of smart cities.

## FACTORS POSING CHALLENGES TO SMART CITIES DEVELOPMENT

Bawany and Shamsi (2015) in the quest to explain the key challenges of smart cities highlighted some factors which are discussed below.

### Information Technology (IT) Infrastructure

The improvement of Information Communication Technology (ICT) foundation from correspondence channels to sensors and actuators in physical space remains a gigantic boundary in taking a keen city activity. The absence of framework is a critical boundary in accomplishing shrewd city destinations. Dependable, versatile and rapid system availability and framework is a key establishment for coordinating data frameworks crosswise over city. This framework must be set up before keen city administrations are offered to partners. Thus, the sufficient dependable IT framework which has a tendency to be adaptable is a basic test for the execution of keen city.

### Security and Privacy

The security in this context inherently implies the weakness of information to either inadvertent or ponder ruptures which can be caused because of authoritative or specialised disappointments. Edwards (2015) made it clear that cities and frameworks are the most complex structures which have ever been made by men, yet when these urban communities and foundation turn out to be so dependent on coordinated correspondence framework and remote sensor systems. This makes them more inclined and defenceless against control disappointment (particularly in a nation like Nigeria where it is so hard to have a 24 hours light in any piece of the nation), programming mistakes and digital assault. The absence of dependability and security of Internet-of-Things (IoT) has made the powerlessness and uncertainty of savvy city frameworks a recognised marvel.

For smart cities development, the key challenges of Smart city are prone to multiplying by the complexities engaged with various merchants and interoperating frameworks; and the impacts might be significant all the more decimating. Cerrudo (2014) opined that new innovations been executed by most urban areas are with next to zero digital security testing. For instance, traffic control sensors introduced in Washington DC, and some different urban areas can be effortlessly hacked with a basic adventure modified on modest equipment.

Brown (2014) asserted that the vulnerabilities of shrewd urban communities will be difficult to deliver offered connections to more seasoned open and private part frameworks. Vulnerabilities and uncertainty in implanted structures cannot be as basically fixed carefully as traditional programming, prompting a conceivable eventual fate of the 'Web of Junk' – to put it plainly, shrewd urban areas are a security catastrophe holding up to happen (Edwards, 2015).

There are three driving wellsprings of mechanical danger to protection as opined by Edwards (2015), which has contended that the brilliant city is the area for an 'immaculate tempest' conjunction of innovative dangers to security. These are: the IOT, Big Data and the Cloud.

Big Data management is one of the major problems of Smart cities as opined by Bawany and Shamsi (2015) and this will be discussed as a broader topic.

### *The IoT*

The IoT, otherwise called universal registering, unavoidable figuring or encompassing knowledge has a long history in software engineering. It has however as of late gone to the consideration of legal advisors. As characterised by Pew Research Internet Project (2014), IoT is a worldwide, immersive, undetectable, surrounding arranged registering condition worked through the proceeded with the expansion of savvy sensors, cameras, programming, databases and enormous server farms in a world-spreading over data texture. It is currently more than a long time since the quantity of 'things' associated with the Internet surpassed the number of individuals. Desires in 2013–2014 for a few things that will be associated with the Internet by 2020 change basically, with Gartner (2015) anticipating 25 billion and Cisco citing 50 billion, however, there is a general assertion that the IoT will be a noteworthy element of our future social orders. In Gartner (2015), shrewd urban areas are one of the critical parts for drawing in interest in the IoT space.

There is a developing pattern of the potential risk the IoT postures to the protection and expanding open attention to the IoT, particularly in the keen city setting, as an apparatus for unavoidable observation. When we share individual information in the advanced online world – for instance, on Google, Facebook, eBay or Amazon, we are straightforwardly or in a roundabout way mindful of intersection a limit into the area of that stage, and intermittently we have chances to give or withhold our agree to information gathering, before we begin to utilise the administration (regardless of the possibility that indeed our primary alternative is either to take or entirely dismiss the administration). In the IoT, such notices and opportunities are transcendently missing by the outline. Indeed, even where unpretentiousness is not a capacity determination, IoT gadgets just do not for the most part have intends to show security sees as well as to intends to give adjusted assent in accordance with the inclinations communicated by people, as gadgets are generally screened less, little or do not have an information instrument (a console or a touchscreen). The issue is awful in residential homes and deteriorates in the general population spots of bright urban areas. While buyers may, at any rate, have hypothetically had an opportunity to peruse the protection approach of their Nest indoor regulator before marking the agreement, they will have no such open door in any genuine sense when the shrewd street gathers their information they go to chip away at, or as they pass the savvy squander canister in the road.

### *The Cloud*

The vast majority of the information created in keen urban communities should be put away in the cloud. Subsequently, the boundless utilisation of distributed computing for accepting and handling data from the shrewd IoT gadgets and applications along these lines raises legitimate prickly issues spinning around locale and physical law. Distributed computing is ordinarily in light of the arrangement of assets to clients from a system of servers and of suppliers and sub-suppliers, with information stockpiling, programming and foundation all made progressively accessible as an administration.

### *Big Data Management*

It is reasonable that from all keen city frameworks, a tremendous measure of information will be created and there is no guarantee to an abnormal state of information quality. Treatment of different sorts of this information with the end goal of openness for business insight and enormous information investigation applications requires proficient huge information administration framework which must be versatile with no downtime and furthermore solid. Rouse (2013) discussed that the effective information administration encourages associations and organisations to find significant data in the substantial arrangement of unstructured information and semi-organised information from an assortment of sources, including, framework logs, call detail records and web-based social networking destinations.

There is a challenge in ceaseless age, gathering, preparing and capacity of monstrous heterogeneous information from endless keen city sensors, in any case, enormous information gathered crosswise over the city is greatly helpful and is fundamental for accomplishing the goal of smart city.

## Cost

Enormous IT infrastructure is required by smart city and there is need for a huge financial investment in order to put the system in place. Several computing devices and networking equipment will be needed to get adequate end-to-end connectivity. There will be great mount of cost to be expended on the requirements of IT professional and consultancies service. The investment in not only constrained to a singular time as operational and maintenance cost which will also amount to a higher expenses will required for such a huge real time system. In order to meet more efficiency requirement and stringent reliability, more resources will also be required leading to a huge amount of overheads. Here is a great example:

> *In case of smart traffic management system each car has to fitted with a sensors and thousands of road side units must be installed. Such system cannot afford a downtime and must be highly efficient and reliable. In a typical urban city, cost of implementing such a project may be around millions of dollars. (Bawany & Shamsi, 2015)*

## Efficiency, Availability and Scalability

Downtime cannot be afforded especially with critical systems and when high availability is required but meeting the availability requirements is tough and directly proportional to the size of the system and its complexity. Smart city do not only have a very huge infrastructure but also have the ability to increase its size and complexity as it goes operational. The un-exhaustive data that are generated across the city will make scalability, availability and efficiency a serious challenge.

The main obligation is to maintain the efficiency of this gigantic system. Some key benefits of smart city can be outlined as proficient planning, immediate response and efficient utilisation of resources and performance optimisation of each system. For example, there is tendency for diverse civil departments impart promptly with one another during the time of crisis which will result to quick access to emergency services. Also, projects for cities can be initiated well before demand for the projects crosses supply and resources requirement can also be consequently calculated. A good example is the calculation of energy requirement through smart grid which enables government to plan to meet the prerequisites for the upcoming year before it comes and also before it goes critical. For a better maximisation of the productivity of current resources, smart grid can be put in place and architectural scalability should be the characteristics of this type of system – such system where management, analytical requirement and data processing will excessively increase. This will definitely compromise the throughput and response time significantly.

## Social Adaption

The overpopulation problems in the urban areas seems to have a great relieving thought at the emergence of smart city. Researchers have identified inequality, digital divide and changing cultural habits to be the challenges to be faced herewith. Social adaption of this type of system requires some things like changing the social habits of citizen in the locality generally and also city managing people specifically.

## Application Development

Developing innovative and new applications speedily and quickly will be required in order for citizens to take the ideal preferred standpoint of information that is being gathered. There is a greater probability that individuals will get frustrated by moderate application improvement if application advancement is restricted to city management. To say however a couple is an instance of the achievement flare-up and wide adaption of Android which can be followed back to its play store, its enormous application base where various applications are been uploaded each day.

## CITIES IN AFRICA

The use of modern innovation could be a huge contributor to reasonable urbanisation in sub-Saharan Africa by enabling urban areas in the district to jump customary procedures of urban improvement and administration. Verifiably, urban improvement has been to a great extent responsive, normally creating answers for issues reflectively, bringing about ease back adjustment to changes in the way individuals live and work. This has brought about astoundingly high adjustment costs and an inheritance of bungle that holds on until today. Numerous urban communities in the creating scene – home to the most quick rates of urbanisation on the planet which are as of now urgently shy of assets, chance rehashing such missteps. Staying away from such a situation in the twenty-first century is fundamental.

We cannot afford to build cities like in the past centuries; commit errors and after that little by little enhance them. Part of the response to this predicament was the proposition that can be found in the utilisation of present-day data innovation, something that the Senseable City Lab activity is effectively engaged with. Through the sending of sensors and handheld observing gadgets throughout transportation, water and waste frameworks, the project is a piece of a more extensive exertion went for creating approaches to map urban areas progressively. The goal is to better comprehend the built environment and utilise such data to create innovative strategies to deal with the process of urbanisation.

African urban areas, for example, Lagos, Cairo and Johannesburg are not just practical on the back of the broadcast communications transformation that has swept the continent in the most recent decade as indicated by IBM's, but they are fundamental towards its practices.

Incorporating innovations into policy planning on the continent could address what is generally perceived to be one of the greatest obstacles to manageable urbanisation in infrastructure. Sub-Saharan Africa is a ready market to be explored in infrastructural development. At present, just to adapt to existing necessities, the locales are locked with a yearly deficiency of near $50bn of speculation into transport, power, water supply and sanitation. With the urban populace in Africa set to dramatically multiply in the coming decades, decreasing that cost will be basic. By enabling business and approach creators to not just utilise assets all the more effectively, the capacity to plan more proactive strategies around urbanisation can on a fundamental level drastically lessen the cost related with the administration of the urban space.

Experts in Kenya, for instance, understand that they have a chance to jump a portion of the inheritance frameworks that exist in the created world. In other developing markets and creating nations, city organisers are looking to what different urban communities in the created countries have done. They would prefer not to rehash the errors.

As part of data innovation in the extension and development of urban communities keeps on developing, it appears certain that it will assume a fundamental part in creating areas especially in Sub-Saharan Africa. Coordinating that innovation in the correct way will be fundamental if urbanisation in the twenty-first century is to be a motor of development in centre and low salary locales, instead of a magnet for imbalance and social disappointment.

## CONCLUSION

The eventual fate of savvy urban areas is essential, they may offer answers for some of our most exceedingly disturbing issues like saving energy and making a supportable situation, keeping up open wellbeing, and safeguarding millennial from despondency and dejection. In urban communities with regions of blended and various hardships, smart city will offer solutions by alleviating some of the hardships through its easy and sustainable developed concepts. While some challenges might hinder the progress of smart city with variance to locations, when these challenges are taken care of, there is always going to be improvement in the overall sector of the city and its immediate environment.

## REFERENCES

Bawany, N. Z., & Shamsi, J. A. (2015). Smart city architecture: Vision and challenges. *(IJACSA) International Journal of Advanced Computer Science and Applications*, *6*(11), 247–255.

Brown, I. (2014). *Regulation and the internet of things (ITU, 2015)* (draft issued for discussion). GSR Discussion Paper. Retrieved from http://www.itu.int/en/ITUD/Conferences/GSR/Documents/GSR2015/Discussion_papers_and_Presentations/GSR_DiscussionPaper_IoT.pdf

Cerrudo, C. (2014). Hacking US (and UK, Australia, France, etc.) traffic control systems. Retrieved from http://blog.ioactive.com/2014/04/hacking-us-and-uk-australia-france_etc.html

Edwards, L. (2015). Privacy, security and data protection in smart cities: A critical EU law perspective. RCUK funded Centre for Copyright and New Business Models in the Creative Economy (CREATe). Retrieved from https://strathprints.strath.ac.uk/55917/1/Edwards_EDPLR_2016_Privacy_security_and_data_protection_in_smart_cities_a_critical_EU.pdf

Gartner. (2015). Hype cycle for the internet of things. Retrieved from https://www.gartner.com/doc/3098434/hype-cycle-internet-things

Millard, C. (2013). *Cloud computing law*. London: Oxford University Press.

Pew Research Internet Project. (2014, May 14). The internet of things will thrive by 2025. Retrieved from http://www.pewinternet.org/2014/05/14/internet-of-things/

Rouse, M. (2013, October). Big data management. Retrieved from http://searchdatamanagement.techtarget.com/definition/big-data-management

# 13

# PROCUREMENT IN SMART CITY DEVELOPMENT

## ABSTRACT

*This chapter discusses the involvement of procurement in smart city development. Procurement plays a vital role in the development of strategies in planning, and execution in the construction industry. This is further introduced into smart city to find the best possible methods of bringing the ideas behind smart city into realisation. The common procurement methods are explained along with their involvement in smart city. Common drawbacks to smart cities procurement and measures to challenges in the procurement of smart city are also explicitly explained in the chapter. Through an identified and accepted procurement method into smart city, the processes involved in executing smart city will be the ones with directions and proper planning.*

**Keywords:** Procurement; procurement management; procurement methods; smart city procurement; sustainability; sustainable development

## INTRODUCTION

There are different terms emerging in the construction industry and its development in present millennium. Most of these emerging innovations are gaining popularity in many developed countries. The immense benefits achieved from the adoption of these innovations gave leeway for it penetration into construction industry of other countries. One of the emerging nomenclatures in construction industry is termed 'smart city'. Smart city had become a topical issue in academic literatures since 1990s (Albino, Berardi, & Dangelico, 2015). However, Glasmeier and Christopherson (2015) opined that smart city can be traced to construction professionals and scholars' intuitive reasoning and projection in the 1980s. Collective brainstorming of what a real city would constitute in future. But there are diverse opinions on what a smart city is and what denotes a city as a smart one. To get proper understanding of smart city, there is a need to unveil what a city is and what constitutes it. Cities can be defined as confinement where large number of people lives, a centre of commerce and transportation with special right to royal and government charter (United Nations, 2016). Geographical boundary for consensus definition of a city is also a topical issue among scholars. Above all, Mori and Christodoulou (2012) submitted that cities play significant role in assessing socio-economic development level of a country. The gradual (though slow) shift from city to smart city calls for identifying procurement methods that best suite achieving the goal in countries of the world. Therefore, this study identifies the procurement methods available in construction industry to synthesise the method used in countries with smart cities element and recommend the suitable procurement method for procurement of smart cities.

## SMART CITY

There have been various views on what a smart city is. Lack of unified consensus on this emerging term has led to confusion among many sectors. It has also brought confusion among urban policy makers as they are making frantic effort in enacting policies that would make their cities smart (Albino et al., 2015). The genesis of smart city can be dated to when developed nations started to make attempt into incorporating information communication technology (ICT) into modern infrastructures. Alawadhi et al. (2012) submitted that California Institute for Smart Communities was the first to gear how major cities could be designed to integrate information technologies. The concept of smart city is based on how a community can be digitised to reflect computer development and yet there has not been an agreed definition (O'Grady & O'Hare, 2012).

The word 'smart' is usable in various context, sector and form. The overall basis centre on a digitised attributes of a particular phenomenon. There have been various words with prefix 'smart' used in some literatures. They include smart industry, smart governance, smart education, smart community, smart people, etc. (Giffinger & Pichler-Milanovíc, Giffinger & Pichler-Milanovíc,

2007). ICT industries are predominantly smart industry. Other industries with information technology production process or techniques are termed smart industry also. Giffinger and Pichler-Milanovíc (2007) defined smart city as a city that is designed to incorporate new technologies in its day-to-day activities with proper monitoring of all the digitised designed features. Smart city cut across modern transportation technologies that improve mobility of residents in the city, security, energy conservation, sustainable development, green structures, etc.

Smart city is described as such that has the six major performing arms that an environment or a geographic location can be summarised with. The completeness of a succinct definition of smart city must reflect the calibres of people domiciled in the area, the prevailing economy, people oriented governance, technologically oriented mobility, geographical environment and the standard of living of the people (Giffinger & Pichler-Milanovíc, 2007). These arms or characteristics emanate from smart combination of endowment and self-decisive operations coupled with awareness of the citizen in the community or city. The six parts identified by Giffinger and Pichler-Milanovíc (2007) are outcome of findings but the pattern and hierarchy are not conclusive.

## PROCUREMENT

Acquisition of public construction products is often birthed by systematic techniques termed procurement. Procurement to a lame man is the process involved in obtaining a good or services. But in construction work parlance, Cartildge (2009) defined procurement as a process involved in obtaining the whole spectrum of goods, materials, plant and services in order to design, build and commission a building that delivers the best possible value for money for client over its life cycle. Ramus, Birchall, and Griffiths (2006) defined construction procurement as overall process and procedure undertaken in achieving a building, infrastructure or professional services rendered. Procurement has various methods with which a client can key into in achieving the delivery of services required. The various methods give the client various choices of management structures, different contractual arrangement and varying degree of clients' risk (Ramus et al., 2006).

Decision as to the type of construction procurement method to employ is a function of the type of client (public or private sector) and the type of construction work to be undertaken (new or refurbishment work). Both public and private clients have been observed to have preferred construction procurement method, which is a function of the requirement expected by each client. Public clients emphasise transparency and accountability while private clients emphasise is majorly on actualising the end-product, that is, it is less regulated as public sector. Traditional procurement methods is gradually fading out as clients desired that construction works should start early and possibly involve participation of several members. This leads to management contracting in the 1970s, partnering, alliance, etc. Brook (2008) observed that the desire of client for procurement methods which could quickly produce (or refurbish) large buildings with complex designs started around late 1980s. The need for contractor's involvement in design phase of construction work and continuous advice on design throughout the construction phase became evident around this time also. Projects with less complex design and build systems also need to be adopted for quick delivery. All these birthed the need for a more proactive procurement system in the construction industry. Advocate for reform in public procurement became topical issue in twentieth century as a result of changing clients' need. However, contract related changes have been observed in Nigeria since 1960s.

## BRIEF ON PUBLIC PROCUREMENT

Public procurement is an arm of government with important function for several reasons. Callendar and Mathews (2000) submitted that financial estimate of government procurement is 10–30% of the gross national product. Public procurement is also an important tool for achieving economic, social and other objectives (Thai, 2001). However, Nakamura (2004) perceived element of waste and corruption in public procurement processes. Overcoming this perception is a great challenge in public procurement all over the world.

There are certain rules and regulations guiding public procurement process. One of which is the number of days with which advertisement of a public contract should not be less than 40 days from the day of publication to the deadline of tender submission. However, there are certain cases of having a shorter period of 10–24 days (Thai, 2001).

## PUBLIC PROCUREMENT SYSTEM

Procurement system is expected to satisfy two basic requirements: management requirement and policy requirement. Procurement management requirement include quality, timeliness, cost (not a mere price), technical risk, maximising business competitiveness and maintaining integrity. While the policy procurement requirement include economic goal (preferring domestic and local firms), environmental protection or green procurement (promoting the use of recycled goods), social goals (assisting minority and woman – owned business concerns) and international trade agreement. Fig. 13.1 shows the interaction in the procurement system with the feedback one of the most essential aspect of the system. Regulation, management and decision making, functional operation and authorisation and selection makes up the other part of the system represented.

## PROCUREMENT METHODS

Ogunsanmi, Iyagba, and Omirin (2003) described procurement method as systematic means that organise technique and approach for achieving a goal of acquisition of a substance or entity. In construction project parlance, project procurement refers to organised methods or process and procedure of actualising a construction product. Procurement process connotes complete cycle of processes from the identification of need through to the completion of the contract.

There are various procurement methods in construction industry. It ranges from traditional methods to non-conventional methods of procurement which include the design and build, project management, construction management,

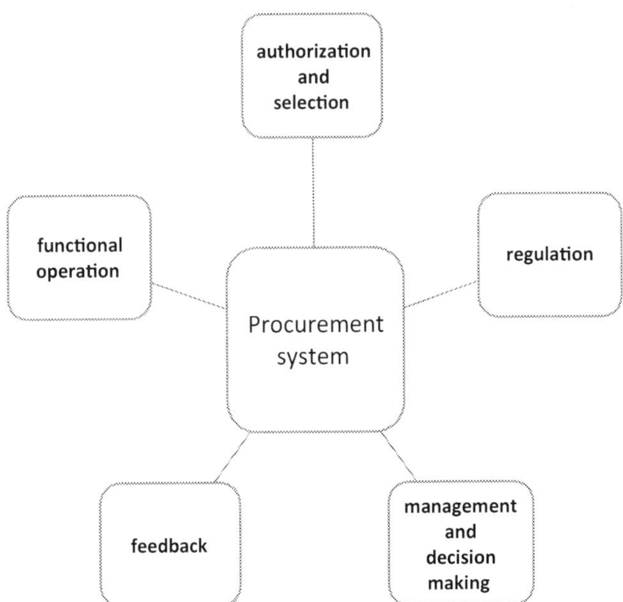


**Fig. 13.1. Public Procurement System.**

management contracting, labour-only, direct-labor and other discretionary procurements such as alliancing, partnering and joint ventures (Babatunde, Opawole, & Ujaddaghe, 2010; Dada, 2012; Ibiyemi, Adenuga, & Odusami, 2008; Ogunsanmi et al., 2003; Ojo, Adeyemi, & Fagbenle, 2006).

The procurement method is divided into five which includes:

1. Traditional procurement method.
2. Construction management procurement method:
    - i. Construction management.
    - ii. Management contracting.
3. Single source procurement method:
    - i. Design and build method.
    - ii. Package deal method.
    - iii. Turnkey method.
4. Collaborative procurement method:
    - i. Partnering.
    - ii. Public private partnership.
    - iii. Joint ventures.
    - iv. Strategic alliance.
5. Fast track procurement method.

## PROCUREMENT OF SMART CITIES

Smart cities are technology based and innovative infrastructures. In a conference organised in Vietnam toward knowledge based society, it was noted that procurement is a strategic tool in stimulating innovation in construction industry and processes. Hence, the procurement method must be carefully selected in order to achieve the aim of the project. There are key characteristics of innovative procurement methods. The characteristics include:

1. The need for leaders (project sponsor or client and other stakeholders) to identify smart cities development need advanced procurement method.

2. Such procurement needs experienced organisations with experienced staff and centralised process management.
3. The procurement involves taking of risk which is majorly bore by the constructor. Hence, the organisation must be equipped enough to tackle all risk that could be envisage in the course of construction.
4. Value for money is a critical factor in this kind of procurement. What constitute value must be clearly stated from onset. Lowest bid is not as critical has having value statement understood by all bidders.
5. Public administration and smart cities provider needs to collaboratively participate in ensuring that stated objectives are achieved.

## COMMON DRAWBACKS TO SMART CITIES PROCUREMENT

Smart city is one of the emerging innovations in construction industry. Driving this innovation in the required way definitely need high level of professional expertise and sound training that is insufficient among many procurement officers. Clarke (2017) submitted that United Kingdom (UK) in its development and level of technology advancement does not have such technical procurement officer that can develop procurement of smart city. This submission was based on premise of grading and paying ground for civil servant in procurement unit. Hundreds of English civil servants were graded and their pay altered following a series of high-profile procurement mistakes. The little number of procurement officers in UK with technical capability and willingness to acquire and explore more innovative procurement processes and methods are hindered by European Union (EU) procurement rules. The EU procurement rules are denoted with lack of drive that propels innovation. This has limited procurement officers' zeal and zest for emerging innovative methods of procurement.

Procurement of a smart city is an innovative endeavour that is termed intellectual property (IP). Eduardo Martínez Gil, a consultant at the Indra Centre of Excellence for Smart Cities identified the question of who owns the IP when the project is finally completed and identified that as a major barrier to local authorities putting in mind that the local authorities (governments at all level) are major driver of innovative projects. The IP in this context is not that of the final product, but all the processes (technologies and expertise) that goes into making the product. Clarke (2017) also revealed that most times the IP on smart cities projects is very complex to define.

## MEASURES TO CHALLENGE OF PROCUREMENT OF SMART CITY

Another gap in procurement emerging innovation like smart city is thin line between research push and market pull. Thus, it makes marketing of innovative solution very difficult. To bridge this gap in Vietnam, various funding schemes are provided to strengthen research development. An increasing number of expert groups recommend complementing public funding for research and innovation by new measures to strengthen the market pull for innovation. A continuous monitoring process has been set up. Studies are foreseen to check obstacles and good practices for the public procurement of innovation.

## CONCLUSION

The world is going smart and the need to underpin level procurement of smartness is imperative. This study reveals that procurement of smart city is relatively low. No procurement method is described best for construction projects in smart city because of different factors that are attached in executing the project. The low level of procurement of smart city could be due to the fact that smart city is an emerging concept. However, the features of various procurement methods can be used as a benchmark to recommend the suitable procurement method for construction works.

## REFERENCES

Alawadhi, S., Aldama-Nalda, A., Chourabi, H., Gil-Garcia, J. R., Leung, S., Mellouli, S., Nam, T., Pardo, T.A., Scholl, H.J. and Walker, S. (2012). Building understanding of smart city initiatives. Berlin, Germany: Springer. https://doi.org/10.1007/978-3-642-33489-4_4

Albino, V., Berardi, U., & Dangelico, R. M. (2015). Smart cities: definitions, dimensions, performance, and initiatives. *Journal of Urban Technology*, *22*(1), 3–21. doi:10.1080/10630732.2014.942092

Babatunde, S. O., Opawole, A., & Ujaddaghe, I. C. (2010). An appraisal of project procurement method in the Nigerian construction industry. *Civil Engineering Dimension*, *12*(1), 1–7.

Brook, M. (2008). *Estimating and tendering for construction work*. Oxford: Elsevier Butterworth-Heinemann.

Callendar, G., & Mathews, D. (2000). Government purchasing: An evolving profession?. *Journal of Public Budgeting, Accounting & Financial Management*, 12(2), 272–290.

Cartildge, D. (2009). *Quantity surveyor's pocket book*. Oxford: Elsevier Butterworth-Heinemann.

Clarke O. (2017). *Smart cities in Europe: Can public procurement be used as leverage to drive smart city solution?*. Smart Cities in Europe Series Report, pp. 1–8.

Dada, M. O. (2012). A second look: Stakeholders' perceptions of some issues in design bid-build procurement practice in Nigeria. *Journal of Sustainable Development*, 5(1), 55–63.

Giffinger, R., & Pichler-Milanovíc, N. (2007). *Smart cities: Ranking of European medium sized cities*. Vienna: Centre of Regional Science, Vienna University of Technology. Retrieved from http://www.smartcities.eu/download/smart_cities_final_report.pdf

Glasmeier, A., & Christopherson, S. (2015). Thinking about smart cities. *Cambridge Journal of Regions, Economy and Society*, 8, 3–12.

Ibiyemi, A. O., Adenuga, A. O., & Odusami, K. T. (2008). Comparative analysis of design and build and the traditional procurement methods in Lagos, Nigeria. *Journal of Construction*, 2(2), 2–6.

Mori, K., & Christodoulou, A. (2012). Review of sustainability indices and indicators: Towards a new city. Sustainability Index (CSI). *Environmental Impact Assessment Review*, 32(1), 94–106.

Nakamura, D. (2004). Untrained staffers blamed for costing city thousands. *Washington Post*, p. B01, Washington, United States.

O'Grady, M., & O'Hare, G. (2012). How smart is your city?. *Science*, 335, 1581–1582. doi:10.1126/science.1217637

Ogunsanmi, O. E., lyagba, R. O. A., & Omirin, M. M. (2003). A comparative study of the performance of traditional and labour-only procurement in Nigeria. *Journal of the Nigerian Institute of Builders*, 2(2), 12–27.

Ojo, S. O., Adeyemi, A. Y., & Fagbenle, O. I. (2006). The performance of traditional contract procurement on housing projects in Nigeria. *Civil Engineering Dimension*, 8(2), 81–86.

Ramus, J., Birchall, S., & Griffiths, P. (2006). *Contract practice for surveyors*. Oxford: Elsevier Butterworth-Heinemann.

Thai, K. V. (2001). Public procurement re-examined. *Journal of Public Procurement*, *1*(1), 9–50.

United Nations. (2016). The sustainable development goals report. Retrieved from https://www.un.org/development/desa/publications/the-sustainable-developmentgoals-report-2016.html

# INDEX

Printed in the United States
by Baker & Taylor Publisher Services